The *City of Ottawa*

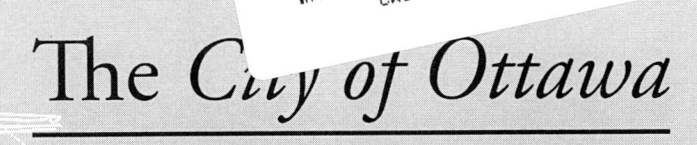

THE STORY OF A SAILING SHIP

by
Judith Samuel MA MCIL

Copyright © 2015 Judith Samuel
Published by Penlan Publishing 2015
Penlan Publishing, 6 Seabank Road, Rhyl LL18 1EA
www.penlanpublishing.com
First printed 2012
Second impression 2014
This edition 2015

The right of Judith Samuel to be identified as the author of this work has been asserted by her in accordance with the Copyright, Designs and Patents Act 1988.
All rights reserved. No part of this publication may be reproduced, stored in a retrieval system, or transmitted in any form or by any means, electronic, mechanical, photocopying, recording or otherwise, without the prior permission of the copyright owner.

ISBN 978-0-9574939-1-9
Typesetting by Crumps Barn Studio.
Printed in Great Britain.

To all the forgotten merchant seamen who sailed on her

Contents

	Page
Introduction	1
Chapter 1 – Life of a Ship: First Years	5
Shipbuilding	5
A Note on the Shipbuilder and Ship's Agent:	6
First Voyage	11
1861–2	14
A Note on Navigation	16
The *Carrier Dove* Incident	17
Chapter 2 – Life of a Ship: Heyday with John Barrett	27
1863	27
A Note on the Second Owners — Thomas Restarick and Thomas Brown Restarick	29
1864–5	31
A Note on Plymouth	32
1866–7	33
A Note on Communications	36
1868–9	36
A Note on Food	37
Chapter 3 – Life of a Ship: Crimps and Collisions	41
1869 continued	41
Danger of Pirates	42
A Note on the Ship's Officers	43
1870	46
A Note on Cardiff	46
Chapter 4 – Life of a Ship: Drunkenness, Theft and Smoking	51
1871	51
1872	52
1873	56
A Note on Newcastle	56
1874 – from 'ship' to 'barque'	59

Chapter 5 – Life of a Ship: Middle Years — 63
   1874 continued — 63
   A Note on Crew Numbers — 63
   1875 — 64
   1876 — 64
   A Note on Liverpool — 65
   1877–8 — 67
   1879 — 68
   Held up by Gales — 70
   1880 — 71
   A Note on Wages — 72
   1881 — 74
   1882 — 74
   1883–4 — 75
   A Note on Sailing Routes — 79
   1885 — 80
   1886 — 81
   1887 — 82

Chapter 6 – Life of a Ship: Old Age and Decline — 87
   1888 — 87
   A Note on the Port of Quebec — 88
   1889 — 90
   1890 — 92
   1891 — 92
   1892–5 — 93
   1896–7 — 93
   1897 – 1905 — 96
   1906 — 96

Chapter 7 – Two Masters, One Mate — 103
   Two Masters — 103
   — John Barrett — 103
   Masters' and Mates' Certificates — 104
   — Henry Pinhey — 106
   — William and George Barrett and Frederick and Frank Pinhey — 114
   One Mate — 115
   — William Bunker — 115

Chapter 8 – The Crew — 119
- Apprentices and 'Boys' — 119
- Ordinary Seamen and Able Seamen — 121
- Age — 122
- Country of Origin — 122
- Sociability — 123
- Literacy — 124
- Possessions — 124
- Conditions — 126

Chapter Nine – Crime, Misdemeanours and Punishment — 129
- Stowaways, and other passengers — 129
- Enlisting and deserting — 130
- — Signing on — 131
- — Shipping Masters, Crimps and Coercion — 132
- *Crimps and Quebec* — 133
- — Causes of Desertion — 134
- — The Master and Desertion — 135
- — Leaving legitimately — 136
- Crime and Misdemeanours — 137
- — The Police — 137
- — A Bad Press — 138

Chapter 10 – Illness, Accident and Wellbeing on the *City of Ottawa* — 141
- The Ship Captain's Medical Guide — 142
- Scurvy — 143
- Accidents — 144
- Fevers, Agues … — 145
- Various Other Problems — 148
- Illness as Excuse — 149
- Drunkenness — 149
- Sexually Transmitted Diseases — 150
- Causes of Death Among the Crew — 151
- — Deaths at Sea — 151
- — Deaths on Land — 152
- — Time of Death Unknown — 152

Conclusions	152
CHAPTER 11 – CONCLUSIONS	157
Ordinary Seamen	157
Masters	158
Financial Success	158
And Finally ...	159
BIBLIOGRAPHY	160
INDEX	163

Figures

		Page
Figure 1:	View over suburban Quebec: can you spot the shipbuilding yards? *Reproduced courtesy of Bibliothèque et Archives nationales du Québec Cliche de L-Prudent Vallée S-12, Fiche 14813*	8
Figure 2:	Detail of the above photograph showing five shipbuilding yards along the St Charles river. The Gingras yard was the middle one. *Reproduced courtesy of Bibliothèque et Archives nationales du Québec Cliche de L-Prudent Vallée S-12, Fiche 14813*	9
Figure 3:	Plan of the *Carrier Dove* incident, showing how far the vessel strayed, and also giving some idea of the complexity of the Liverpool Dock system at that time.	18
Figure 4:	Scale of provisions to be allowed and served out to the crew during the voyage	39
Figure 5:	Map of the voyage of the *City of Ottawa* in 1872/3, to Italy and Burma	52
Figure 6:	Boats at Sharpness, showing rafts of timber in the foreground. *Reproduced courtesy of Gloucestershire Archives, ref. SR9/49274*	65
Figure 7:	Map of the *Ottawa*'s longest voyage, 1883/4	76
Figure 8:	Plan from 1896 showing the proposed position for the *City of Ottawa*, identified as 'explosives hulk'. *Image courtesy of the National Archives, ref. ADM1/7279.*	95
Figure 9:	Photograph of the Robert Jones Shipbuilding Yard in Rhyl in 1870. *Reproduced courtey of Flintshire Archives, ref: PH/56/261*	97

Figure 10: The *Fearless* beached on a sandbank, to the entertainment of holidaymakers.   98

Figure 11: Rhyl harbour in 1900, just before the *Ottawa* arrived there. *Reproduced courtesy of Flintshire Archives, ref: PH/56/412*   98

PLATES

Plate i: The remains of the *City of Ottawa* in Rhyl harbour

Plate ii: The St Charles River today, from the approximate site of the Gingras yard

Plate iii: A scale model of the *City of Ottawa*, made by carpenter Jeremy Brookes

Plate iv: A scroll figurehead, perhaps similar to that of the *City of Ottawa*

Plate v: The *City of Ottawa* today, showing the 'iron knees' (ignore the shopping trolley to the left, this is not original!)

Plate vi: An original painting of the *City of Ottawa*, made in 1860 to facilitate her first sale. *Reproduced courtesy of the Collection of the Maritime Museum of the Atlantic, Halifax, Nova Scotia, Canada*

Plate vii: The Northumberland Arms, once a Seaman's Hostel

Plate viii: A double-front-doored house in North Shields, similar to the one where the Melrose family had an apartment

Plate ix: A modern picture of Gloucester Docks. The vessel shown is of similar dimensions to the *City of Ottawa*, which gives an idea of her size

Plate x: Liverpool Docks: the Albert Dock, which the *City of Ottawa* visited several times

Plate xi: The house where John Barrett grew up, by the water's edge at Stonehouses, Plymouth

Plate xii: Plan from 1878 showing Henry Pinhey's riverside plot on the Isle of Orleans, Quebec. *Reproduced courtesy of the Bibliothèque et Archives nationales du Québec Ref. CA301 Fonds Cour supérieure. District judiciaire de Québec. Greffes d'arpenteurs (Québec) S48 Alexander Sewell (l'arpenteur): E21 S80 SS1 SSS4 PD 088.*

Plates xiii – xv: The three suicide notes left by Henry Pinhey. *Reproduced courtesy of Bibliothèque et Archives nationales du Québec Ref. Enquêtes du Coroner TL31 S26 SS1 Fonds Cour des sessions generals de la paix du district de Québec, Dossier no. 26 1901 No. 26*

Plates xvi – xvii: Two of the houses where the Pinhey family had an apartment. The second building is rather less grand than the first.

Introduction

The remains of the *City of Ottawa* can still be seen in Rhyl Harbour (Plate i), for the time being safe beneath the sandbank, hopefully waiting for a time when there will be enough money to finance further excavation. Researching the history of the vessel has been like embarking on an exciting voyage, as exciting as any of those of the vessel herself.

We tend to honour our Royal Navy vessels like the *Victory* above the merchant fleet, whose history is more often ignored. So not only was the *City of Ottawa* a merchant vessel, but she was not even a famous one like the *Cutty Sark*, nor she did sail for any of the important Shipping Lines like the White Star Line. So why study the *City of Ottawa*? For me there are many reasons: her visible remains are of interest to the archaeologist and casual passerby alike, and a signboard on the other side of the harbour gives some indication of her significance. She was a good honest working ship that sailed commercially for 36 years, well over the average, and then continued to have a useful life for another ten. While we respect the abilities of our famous Admirals like Nelson, we tend to undervalue both historically and currently the skills, abilities, intelligence and talent of the working man. Merchant sailors did not get a good press then, and we tend to repeat the prejudices of the past now. We have a lot of preconceptions about life in the merchant navy, but these are not always based on hard facts. By looking in depth at the records as they relate to one ship, we can test received ideas. We cannot really come to conclusions about all merchant ships (as the sample size is too small), but we can find out a very great deal about one of them.

There was already quite a considerable amount of documentation on the *City of Ottawa*, as well as a preliminary published article by Ian Brown and Fiona Gale[1], and two recent archaeological reviews[2]. Some of the logbooks and crew lists have survived and give a great deal of information, but then annoyingly don't give quite enough. The 'crew lists' are the Ship's Articles, which set out the parameters of the ship's voyage and conditions on ship, with regard to food to be provided, numbers of crew etc. They had to be read out to the men, and each seaman had to sign them, or make his mark if he couldn't sign his own name, and a record was kept of when he was discharged, deserted etc. It was essential to keep the ship's articles up to date and accurate, as they could be used as evidence in legal cases if the seaman wanted to sue for discharge for non-payment of wages for example. Hence they give a lot of useful information about the age and place of birth of the seaman, country of origin, previous ship, date and place of joining current ship, and how and when he left. Logbooks record incidence of sickness, accidents, insubordination and crime for similar reasons, and to a certain extent the vessel's route can be plotted by the bearings given, but they do not usually record cargo, weather conditions or profits made, which would all have been helpful information to have.

So to test the accuracy of the statements that are sometimes made, about the rootlessness of seamen, the drunkenness, the dangers they were subject to, about whether they are moved from ship to ship as the helpless pawns of crimps or boarding house keepers or whether they exerted a fair amount of individual decision-making in following their career, a combination of in-depth analysis and intelligent interpretation (plus the dogged determination of Sherlock Holmes) has been necessary.

The abundance of documentation enhances the interest of the vessel for the social historian. Using the good new genealogical tools, often online, and by dint of some determined digging, it has been possible to find out a lot not only about the vessel's voyages, but about the men who sailed on her. The more I have looked into their lives, the more interesting and fascinating it became, and showed that preconceptions and received ideas on the sort of people who sailed in these ships were not always correct. I would come to a conclusion, only to have to revise this in the light of further information, or a more in depth look at the details given in the crew lists and logbooks. All helped to build up a detailed picture of the working life, collisions, problems, good times and bad, of this fascinating ship, and thus of the merchant navy throughout the Victorian Age. For the timeline of the vessel (1860 – 1906) reflects that of the Queen Victoria herself (1838 – 1901).

But while the documentation pleases the social historian, the physical remains are of considerable interest to archaeologists and maritime historians, for very few vessels built in Canada in the 1860s remain around the world for investigation[3]. The 2007 Report by Gifford suggests 'a significant value for the vessel'[4]. Moreover Wessex Archaeology concluded in 2011 in an unpublished

Introduction

report, "*The site can be considered to be important for a number of reasons. Named to celebrate Queen Victoria's choice of the new Canadian capital just three years before the vessel was completed, the City of Ottawa is one of the best and last remaining examples of a 19th century Quebec-built wooden sailing ship. The vessel was involved in both the Quebec timber trade and probably the Welsh coal trade – industries that defined the economic development of these two areas. The vessel's voyages are well documented, and provide a rich source of information regarding the social history of life on board a 19th century merchant sailing vessel. Finally, the location of the City of Ottawa shipwreck in Foryd Harbour provides an easily accessible visible reminder of the once vibrant shipbuilding and ship-breaking industry of the Rhyl and Foryd waterfronts in the late 19th and early 20th century.*"[5] She was constructed at a time when methods were changing radically as the balance dipped away from sail and towards steam power.

The vessel has even more significance, perhaps, in Canada. In 2007 there was an attempt to have her excavated with the intention of sending some of the remains over there. Rainer Bloess, still Councillor for the Innes Ward, contacted Richard Gimblett, President of the Canadian Nautical Research Society, to lay claim to some of the remains. He believed that the wood used in her construction came from the pine forest in the Ottawa Valley, and that as she was named to commemorate the Canadian capital it was important to preserve them as part of the city's patrimony. However potential funding fell through, and the vessel lies patiently waiting for more to found.

Some of the questions we will examine include:

- Is it true that sailors lived uncomfortable lives, and died young?
- Were they rootless and irresponsible, prey to whim and easy victim of the unscrupulous?
- Was shipowning profitable?
- Did either officers or men do well financially out of it?

Hopefully these issues will become clearer throughout the book.

My project also had an artistic facet, as it was funded by Arts Council Wales and in addition to carrying out historical research I created a body of artwork, which was seen at Rhyl Library from 4th August to 22nd September 2012.

In addition, the City of Ottawa is about to sail into new waters, with a French edition of this book, 'Le City of Ottawa, l'histoire un grand voilier en bois' shortly to be published in Quebec by Éditions GID.

In writing it, I am grateful for the support and encouragement of Fiona Gale, Denbighshire County Archaeologist, and Iolo Williams of Arts Council

Wales. Thanks also to Stuart, who proof read, and Lorna Gray, who did an amazing job with the typesetting. Liffey's Tea Room in Rhyl kindly allowed me to sit for hours over a cup of coffee and sandwich while writing this book and must also be mentioned with gratitude.

---

1 'The *City of Ottawa* – the Remains of a Nineteenth Century Full Rigged Ship lying in the Foryd Harbour, Rhyl, North Wales', I Brown and F Gale, Flintshire Historic Society Journal, 2007, pp 87–105

2 'Rhyl Foryd Harbour. An assessment of the wreck – *City of Ottawa*', Gifford, Report No. 14533 RO1a, December 2007. 'Rhyl Foryd Harbour. A survey of the wreck – *City of Ottawa*', Gifford, Report No. 14533 RO3, July 2008

3 'Rhyl Foryd Harbour. An assessment of the wreck – *City of Ottawa*', Gifford, Report No. 14533 RO1a, December 2007

4 ibid, p19

5 Wessex Archaeology (2011) *City of Ottawa*, Foryd Harbour , Rhyl, Denbighshire, North Wales. Undesignated Site Assessment. Unpublished Report. 53111.02-7. pgs i-ii

Chapter 1

LIFE OF A SHIP: FIRST YEARS

SHIPBUILDING

The 1860s were the golden age of Quebec. Timber was cut with axes and floated down the rivers, fixed together in large rafts, to the bays where they would be sorted or sent to the sawmills for cutting into planks, ready to be loaded onto one of the 1395 sailing ships that docked there annually. Shipbuilding was booming, with a plethora of small yards along both sides of the river St. Lawrence and up its tributaries, together with all the associated businesses, sailmakers, carpenters, blacksmiths, painters, not to mention the ships agents and merchants who provided the finance and the network of contacts[1].

It was here that the *City of Ottawa* was built between September 1859 and July 1860 at the yard of Jean-Elie Gingras, one of the smaller but longest lasting and most prolific of the shipbuilders. His yard was located on a bend in the St Charles river, a smaller tributary of the massive St Lawrence, on a sheltered beach with a smithy and one or two sheds, which from surviving images and plans looks pleasingly makeshift. He leased the land in 1850 from the Augustine Sisters of the General Hospital and it is described as being in the St Roch parish, bounded to the North by the low water line of the St Charles river, to the south running to the top of the hill adjoining the fence of the General Hospital lands, to North East by their property, and to the South West by the land called 'la briquerie', a brick-making concern owned in 1865 by one Adams. If we visit it today we can identify the site from old plans, although no trace remains on the ground. In those days the river was meandering (it has since been straightened) and it hardly seems possible that large ships like the *City of Ottawa*, or even larger, could have been launched there (see Figures 1 and 2, below, and Plate ii). However part of the original General Hospital can still be seen, now incorporated in the modern hospital, which is still in use. Although the river was certainly frozen in winter, construction work on the interior of a ship could continue under tarpaulins[2].

Shipbuilding was a highly skilled profession: the Master Shipbuilder worked from a wooden 'half model' (Plate iii). The shipbuilder would discuss the dimensions required with whoever commissioned the vessel, altering the model as needed, then use it to calculate and scale up the dimensions of the finished ship, which to modern eyes looks harder than writing it on paper. In Quebec at that time plans were hardly ever written down[3], and none survive for the *City of Ottawa* (this enhances the archaeological significance of the hulk, which represents the only well preserved vessel of its type built in Quebec at that period, and could provide evidence of construction techniques[4]).

Ships could be built for specific purchasers, but often, like the *Ottawa*, were built speculatively for the British market. Gingras was usually financed by James Gibb Ross, Ship's Agent, and this was what happened in the *Ottawa*'s case. On 26th October 1859[5], Jean-Elie Gingras, this time working with Louis Labbé, a frequent partner of his, raised a mortgage on the ship, which was already under construction. Although the shipyard described is Gingras' usual one, he was acting as attorney to Labbé, who is named as the shipbuilder. Ross is to advance £7 per ton, to be repaid on 1st August 1860 at 5% interest, which was roughly his usual terms. Gingras received any profits from the sale above the price of the loan, plus perhaps profits from shipping the first cargo to Britain when it was sent for sale. However if the loan was not repaid on launching in the water, the Agent would be listed as 'owner' on the Registration Document, which is what happened in this case. The ship is to be finished 'in the best workmanlike manner and with the best of materials, iron kneed and upper fastened up to 12", under the direct supervision of a Lloyds Surveyor and so to be classed at Lloyds A1 for 7 years and to launch as early as possible in July next and complete her ready to sail within 15 days thereafter.' She was to have a 'Quebec outfit'.

A Note on the Shipbuilder and Ship's Agent:

Jean-Elie Gingras, born in 1804 to a family of sailors, passed all his 86 years in Quebec. He also started his career as a sailor but then turned to shipbuilding and built a total of 63 ships over a 33 year period. 1860 – 65 were particular boom years for Quebec, as American shipping was tied up in the American Civil War, and from 1855 – 65 Gingras built two or three ships a year (except for 1858, when he built none), peaking at six in 1864, sometimes alone or with one of his sons, sometimes from 1859 with Louis Labbé, to whom his first wife was related. Each time he would have two or more ships in construction simultaneously, launching them in preference in May, June or July, at the start of the sailing season after the snows were thawed. Although he sometimes built larger ships, the *City of Ottawa* was about the average size for his vessels. According to E. Marcil, Gingras had as many as 100 employees in 1880, and probably laid on more on a temporary basis as needed. Not many of the other shipbuilders lasted as long as he did.

He was also involved in local politics and was married three times in all. His descendants recount that according to family lore he sometimes sent relatives to sea in his ships to keep an eye on things (we will see later that the Restarick family did the same). A nephew was thus sent to Britain where the ship picked up a load of Scotch whiskey to be brought back to Quebec. On the trip back, the nephew died. The crew was afraid that Jean-Elie would accuse them of murder so they put the nephew's body in a barrel of scotch rather than burying him at sea. They landed on the Canary Islands and had a doctor certify that the nephew had died of natural causes. Seems a drastic solution!

James Gibb Ross was the most successful Ship's Agent in Quebec, and Jean-Elie Gingras usually relied on him for finance for his ships. Ross was very experienced, with some 250 ships registered in his name from 1858 – 1885. He was also an exporter of wood in his own right, and large-scale investor in insurance, sawmills, paper mills, and railways[6].

Clearly both parties found it a profitable arrangement. The shipbuilder benefited both from the input of finance, and the agent's experience in financing and maritime markets, while the agent made a valuable investment.

The ship was built under 'special survey'. Canada at that time was still part of the British Empire, and laws benefited English ships made of oak over Canadian ones, which tended to be built of softwoods[7]. These were despised by English legislators despite their advantages - and clearly they could be very durable as the Ottawa's long sailing career and survival to the present indicates. Ships were given a rating by Lloyds according to the standards they were built to, and although English ships could receive up to an A13 rating (A was the best rating, and 13 was the number of years before the vessel required another major survey, and re-rating), only the very best Canadian ships could receive an A10. However under 'special survey', the ships would be inspected constantly during construction, requiring perhaps 40 or 50 visits by the inspector, and their rating could be improved, which in turn increased their selling price. The *Ottawa* received an A7 rating, and the Lloyds' Special Survey report survives[8].

This showed that the vessel was built over the winter of 1859/1860, and was launched at the time specified in the contract, 4th July. The certificate was issued on 24th August, signed by Richard Hoggett, Inspector. The vessel was built mainly of tamarack, a type of larch, with oak keel and keelson, decks of yellow pine and outside planking of rock elm, tamarack, and red pine. Part of the fastenings were of metal, including the 'Cato Miller and Co. patent iron knee riders' with 'Bettley and Co' tails, fitted vertically amidships and diagonally forward and aft, and on the deck beams Cato and Miller and Co. patent solid vertical iron knees. Some of these can still be seen (when silt and water levels are low) on the remaining hulk in Rhyl harbour (Plate v) and their use at this period has been particularly studied by archaeologists[9]. She had a long boat with a 25 ft keel, and a pinnace with a 23 ft keel, and 3 anchors, a Bower iron stock weighing 37 tons, a Bower wooden stock of 32 tons, and a Kedge iron stock of 5 tons. She had twenty-one sails. Six vessels are thought to have been built to the same design[10].

Figure 1: View over suburban Quebec: can you spot the shipbuilding yards?
Reproduced courtesy of Bibliothèque et Archives nationales du Québec Cliche de L-Prudent Vallée S-12, Fiche 14813

Life of a Ship: First Years

Figure 2: Detail of the above photograph showing five shipbuilding yards along the St Charles river. The Gingras yard was the middle one.
Reproduced courtesy of Bibliothèque et Archives nationales du Québec Cliche de L-Prudent Vallée S-12, Fiche 14813

The *City of Ottawa* was named to mark an event in the history of Canada, for in 1857 Queen Victoria chose Ottawa to be the capital. Previously a part of the British Empire, Canada was to gain Dominion status in 1867. According to M. Eileen Marcil, 'The Parliament buildings were in the process of being built in 1860, as Queen Victoria had chosen Ottawa as the site of the new Canadian capital. Moreover, the Prince of Wales came over that year and attended several events in Ottawa, so the city was definitely in the news at the time.'[11]

The launch of a vessel would often be announced in the local papers, although if this happened in the *Ottawa*'s case it has not survived: as Jean-Elie Gingras was of French origin it would have been put in the Francophone press which have not been preserved from that period. Another Gingras ship, the *Burnside*, a smaller barque, was launched at about the same time. In those days the launch was often an event, that people would come to see. There would be a celebration for the workers, with sandwiches, beer, cheese and biscuits, while the builder and his elite guests would go to his offices for something more refined, wine, and so on[12]. Sometimes the vessel was launched fully rigged, with sails ready for setting, sometimes just with a pole set temporarily where the main mast would go, to hang a flag from. The *Ottawa* already had masts and rigging when she received her final Lloyds survey. Ships built for sale in Britain would be sailed across the Atlantic and finished in Britain, with oak fittings for the Captain's cabin, perhaps, and copper sheathing to prevent attack by worms and marine creatures: we know that this happened to the *Ottawa*[13], whose hull was protected by Welsh felt and yellow (Munz) metal.

The years 1850 – 1865 were the heyday of the wooden square rigged merchant sailing ships. They could be built very cheaply in Canada, where the cost of labour and materials was still low, and were still the most economical way of transporting goods and materials. At that time, steamships had been in use for some fifty years but were still expensive to run, and could only be used for comparatively short journeys. As the century progressed they slowly took over.

Owning wooden merchant sailing ships was a very risky business to invest in. As expressed succinctly by Basil Greenhill, "Statistics have not yet been seriously examined, but it seems not unlikely that the wooden square rigged sailing ship, ambling about the coasts and over the seas of the world at an average speed, if she was well designed and equipped, well commanded and well managed, of about 5 miles an hour, and more especially the fast wooden sailing ship sailed fast, was probably the most dangerous vehicle ever regularly used by man." [14]

In addition, the wooden sailing ship was labour intensive. It was a priority to protect the cargo, so caulking was inspected once a year to ensure it was still water-tight, and after a few years at sea the vessel might have to be pumped frequently to ensure the cargo kept dry. Other regular maintenance work included dowsing the decks with water when in a hot climate to make sure they didn't dry out, oiling wooden blocks (in the rigging) with linseed and examining them for cracks, and unrigging and taking down the masts and spars. Vessels carried skilled carpenters and sailmakers so maintenance and repairs could be carried out as required.

Canadian ships of the time were well designed, and utilised the latest rigging techniques developed in New England[15]. From 1860 round sterns were introduced (the *Ottawa* had one), and poop decks were short and wide, without cabins half way along the bridge. Canadian vessels were generally made of softwoods, which were light so that they could carry more and cost less to build[16] (although elsewhere iron vessels were beginning to appear) but from the 1860s started to have iron frames and knees. Although the *Ottawa* was mostly made of timber, 'the frame is diagonally iron plated upon the outside according to Rule Section 62 with plates ¾ x 4½ one pair each end 5/8 x 4 ½, seventeen pairs in number, placed at an angle of 45 degrees and bolted with 1 inch iron[17]. This was in addition to the copper sheathing which was applied after the vessel arrived in Liverpool to protect the ship's hull from worm attack[18]. Details such as furnishing the Master's cabin would also be completed in Britain (all this was what was meant by a 'Quebec outfit'). Canadian ships were still being launched with wooden masts — although the Lloyds survey does not state what material the *Ottawa*'s were made of — but these were sometimes replaced in Britain with iron or steel masts, which were becoming more prevalent by that period[19]. From this time forward many improvements were beginning to be made on deck and in the rigging, with iron wire increasingly used for standing and some running rigging.

Also over this period the average size of the ships built increased, and the shape of hulls was modified too. The ancient tonnage measurement system under the 1773 Act, which had been the basis for estimating dues and taxes, had not taken account of depth and had resulted in deep but wide vessels with blunt bows which were hard to handle and manoeuvre. By the 1860s, the tonnage regulations had been modernised and ships were longer but shallower, with narrower hulls to cut through the waves. They carried less cargo but were still more profitable.

Very few sailing ships were built after about 1871. This was partly due to the opening of the Suez Canal in 1869 (inaccessible to sailing ships), which cut out a large part of the journey to the East Indies for steam. At the same time the creation of the compound engine made steamships more efficient. This in turn created a demand for coal, and Britain was the world's largest exporter, so ironically this also meant that sailing ships remained a good investment until the end of the century, providing virtually free storage and transport for coal to ports such as Aden, where steamers could refuel – the *Ottawa* did in fact do this run a couple of times[20]. But the main cargo she carried was timber, and she would be one of the vessels especially adapted for this trade, with special ports in her bows for unloading.[21]

FIRST VOYAGE

So the *Ottawa* was ready for her maiden voyage.

By July 12th the vessel had entered Hall's boom for loading, taking on 143 tons oak, 39 of elm, 13 of birch, 204 of red and 562 of white pine, 38 of tamarack, 6623 stands of deals, and various pipe staves for C. and J. Sharples and Co[22].

The Master was Samuel James Hatfield. He was born at Arcadia, in Yarmouth, Nova Scotia, in 1825, and so was aged 35. He was 5ft 9in, quite tall for the time, with fair complexion, sandy hair and blue eyes, an attractive combination. He had a complicated tattoo, rather like a fleur de lys, on his right arm. He had gone to sea as a boy in 1838, at the age of 13, and took his Master's exam in Cork in Ireland at the age of 31. He had married Polly back in Arcadia in 1850 and went on to have ten children who grew up there, at least one of which was a Master Mariner in his turn. They were all English (rather than French) speaking, all Church of England, and could all read and write. Samuel continued to sail until at least the age of 48, losing two vessels along the way, but must have done quite well as latterly he sailed on his own account, in a family-owned vessel. Possibly he went on even longer as after Canada got Dominion status he no longer needed to be registered with the British Admiralty. At any rate he lived to the age of 83. One interesting fact that arises from his records is that he travelled as a passenger on a ship to Boston at least twice, presumably to join a ship, which was apparently common practice for mariners.

The Merchant

C. and J. Sharples and Co. was just one of the merchants that the *City of Ottawa* carried cargos for, though she was chartered by them on several occasions. They were timber merchants and shipbuilders based in Quebec, formed in 1854 by John Sharples.

A Note on Scale

To give an idea of her size, the *Ottawa* was roughly the length of five double decker buses laid end to end, roughly the width of four laid side by side, and the hold was roughly as high as 1½ of them.

Loading of the *City of Ottawa* was complete by 31st July and the vessel cleared by customs. At about the same time the first registration was completed, at Quebec on August 3rd.[23] This provided for the sale from James Gibb Ross, the Agent, to Kenneth Dowie and William Forbes, Liverpool merchants, they to have a license to sell her at any port in the United Kingdom valid for 12 months. It also gave further details of the vessel. She was a three masted square rigger, with a round stern, carvel built (which denotes that the hull was formed of planks laid close to the frame to present a smooth exterior, as opposed to 'clinker built' where the planks overlapped) with no gallery, and as figurehead she had scroll-work, which was quite common: an example is given at Plate iv. There was only one deck – she was really only a hollow hold, for maximum storage space for cargo – at a registered tonnage of 884 tons, length of 169 ft, breadth 33 ft, depth of hold 21ft (the actual height including the rigging was of course much higher).

There was a round house (a cabin on the after part of the quarterdeck, for cooking among other things), lockers and forecastle (a space in the bows) as sleeping accommodation for the crew. The Master's accommodation would be tucked into the stern. The Registration document was altered in 1889 after the Tonnage Act of that year caused tax to be calculated differently, and hence the on-board accommodation was listed in more detail. From this, working backwards for the stated tonnage of each area and assuming ceiling heights of 9ft, we can deduce that the Master's cabin was approximately 11ft x 12ft, the sailroom c 20ft x 12ft, the storage space for the bosun c 5ft x 10ft, and the crew sleeping space in the forecastle, c 20ft x 16ft.

It was probably about this time that the two surviving paintings of her were produced. These were really an early form of marketing material, and were created to a fairly stylised formula, but they do give an idea of her appearance. The painting reproduced here shows the vessel running under storm rig, and purports to be off the Skerries at Anglesey, North Wales[24]: see Plate vi. Men are visible on the deck, and details of her scroll figurehead can be seen. She is flying three flags: the flag on her foremast is a civilian Jack (the Union Jack with a white border) which could be flown by merchant ships. The white flag with red edge on the main mast was probably the house flag of Ross & Co. The flag at the stern is the British Red Ensign, flown by Colonial ships (as Canada was still a Colony at that time).

The vessel passed customs at Liverpool on 27th August, and her sale was advertised as taking place on October 4th (see below), but clearly she failed to sell and Dowie decided to send her off to Calcutta with a cargo that he had commissioned himself.

The following classified advertisement appeared in the Liverpool Mercury on Thursday September 27th and October 2nd and 4th 1860[25]

Unless previously disposed of by private treaty. On Thursday next, the 4th October, at 3 o'clock at Cunard, Wilson and Co's salesroom, Exchange, Liverpool, the fine new ship *City of Ottawa*, 871 tons o.m., 884 tons register. Length 169 7/10s feet, breadth 33 7/10s feet, depth 21 3/10s feet. Built at Quebec, and launched in July 1860; classed A1 seven years from 1861; is a very strong and faithfully built vessel, a handsome model, and will carry a large cargo; is copper-fastened, has round house, with after-cabin fitted complete, deck house and topgallant forecastle. This vessel is now in the Sandon Graving Dock completing her classification and being boot-topped and coppered. She will be sold with a very advantageous contract for the above work, the present owners paying all expenses up to the time of entering the dry dock. Apply to Messrs. Kenneth Dowie and Co, Merchants, South John Street, or to Cunard Wilson and Co Brokers.

She was surveyed in November at Liverpool, and on November 8th and 9th was loading at Sandon Dock[26]. Cargos are very rarely given in the Log Book or Crew Lists, although they can be identified from a number of sources including contemporary newspapers and Customs House documents but it hasn't always been possible to find out what was carried, as on this occasion. On November 15th she sailed for Calcutta[27], under a moderate southwesterly wind, with Frederick William Withycombe as Master. There is a surprising amount of information about his life: he was born on 27th September 1806 at Teignmouth, to a seagoing family (his father, William, was a mariner also) and apparently had a brother, or cousin, called William Frederick Withycombe, born 30th October 1808 at the same place. If this is confusing to the modern researcher, it also seems to have muddled the Admiralty administration of the time. Frederick William started as an apprentice at the age of 13, in 1819, whereas William Frederick started as a cabin boy two years later. But both started out on small local ships, sailing initially to Canada, and quickly rising to be Mate at a time before it was necessary to take an examination. Frederick became Master of his own ship at 30, but William was only 23 when he captained the *Micmac*. They sailed in tiny ships: Frederick took the *Ann*, 160 tons, all the way to Sydney in Australia in 1841. William seems to have been the most dynamic: not only did he have his own ship earlier, but he married Ann Dench in June 1836 at St Mary's church, Marylebone, London, while Frederick apparently married her sister Eliza at the same place in January 1838. Eliza had been a witness at Ann's wedding. William and Ann had a daughter, Anne, and had moved to Liverpool by 1850, but Frederick continued living at what may well have been Eliza's family home, 65 Seymore Place in Marylebone, and had four daughters. He was 54 when he took over the *City of Ottawa*.

1861–2

The *Ottawa* arrived in Calcutta on 18th March 1861 and started for home on 15th May. On 13th July, just before the end of the year she was licensed for sale and while on her way back, she was sold to Kenneth McKenzie Dowie himself, having presumably still failed to find another buyer. On 11th November she was registered in Liverpool[28], with the same description of the vessel. The advertisement mentions a deckhouse as well as round house but this is not included in the registration document.

However Frederick William Withycombe had died at sea on 4th August. Unfortunately there is no information on cause of death, but it is tempting to believe that he died of an infectious disease picked up in Calcutta: there is no record of whether other crew members also died. Eliza his wife moved to Liverpool and inherited Frederick's personal effects the next February, to the value of about £300. This would be worth £21,800 today in terms of purchasing power but looked at as an indicator of economic status it would be the equivalent to an inherited wealth in the region of £239,000[29]. William stopped sailing in 1863, but lived to the age of at least 63.

One HA or TA Tucker took over the vessel at St Helena at the end of September, and it took one month to get to Liverpool, but as this voyage was too short to be recorded in the Captain's Register and there are lots of 'Captain Tuckers', it is impossible to identify him. Somehow the *Ottawa* seems to have come in on this occasion unnoticed by Customs, perhaps indicating that Withycombe had failed to find a cargo in Calcutta. By 18th November, the vessel was taking on cargo again, sailing on 24th for Calcutta with Thomas Armitage Jackson as Master and again Dowie was trading on his own behalf.

Captain Jackson was a top class mariner who apparently specialised in fast runs to Calcutta, which indicates what a good reputation the *Ottawa* had at that time. He was then 40 and a Liverpudlian born and bred. He had tattoos, small anchors on his right hand and left wrist, was 5ft 5in, roughly an average height for the time, with a dark complexion, and brown hair and eyes. His father was a boot and shoe maker and so could pay for him to be apprenticed at the age of 16, and he served in the Royal Navy for 11 months early in his career. Because of his experience he was excused from taking the Master's Exam. He had three children with his Liverpudlian wife Maria - William who also became a Master Mariner, Maria, and Thomas, who clearly preferred dry land and became a stationer. When his daughter Maria died in 1933 at the age of 83 (she was then Mrs Williams) the Wallasey and Wirral Chronicle published an obituary[30] which quoted from notes she had written on her exciting life. She does not mention the *City of Ottawa* but gives a graphic account of her time on the *Eliza Bencke* which her father captained next. It seems the family often sailed together, and it is quite likely she and her mother but probably not her two brothers went to Calcutta on this occasion. William was then 15 and may have sailed as an apprentice, Maria was 11 and Thomas 9. In her possibly biased account her father comes across as brave and resourceful but perhaps a little cold: when the family's pet cat disappeared in Calcutta, he surmised that he had been stolen, 'to make a fur cap out of his coat'!

The *Ottawa* arrived in Calcutta on May 20th 1862.

A Note on Navigation

The route that vessels took can to a certain extent be plotted because of the system of sightings at sea. In an age when ships did not carry radios, if they passed each other within hailing distance they would identify themselves and their destination, and on coming to port would report all sightings made in this way, which would be announced in Lloyd's List. This was a way for the owner, relatives etc to get news of the progress the ship was making. On this occasion, the *City of Ottawa* was sighted off the coast of Rio di Janeiro in January: ships going southwards from Britain swung wide across the Atlantic, rounding the Cape of Good Hope off South Africa well to the south, before heading for the East Indies or China.

It has been claimed that the *Ottawa* circumnavigated the globe twenty times, but this does not in fact seem to be correct[31]. Although the Southern Ocean offers the only direct water route right round the globe before the prevailing westerly winds, in fact the sightings indicate that the *Ottawa* generally went to the East Indies passing south of Africa, and came back the same way in reverse. Alan Villiers[32] records that ships could cross the Indian Ocean with a fair wind in the Trade Winds belt, helped past the Cape by the Algulhas current. The ship would steer through the South Atlantic, heading for a point midway between Fernando Noronha and the Cape Verde islands, which gave better Trade Winds and a clear ocean, well away from the Brazil Current which sweeps along the east coast of Brazil, and a fair chance of working through the Doldrums. The Doldrums, called the Horse Latitudes, are a belt of calm around the Equator, where a ship could be held up waiting for a wind. William Lord[33], who first went to sea on merchant ships similar to the *Ottawa* at the age of 13 in the 1860s, later published a book of reminiscences which provide useful firsthand knowledge of the Victorian seafarer's experiences. He records that passing through the Doldrums was a tiring time, when the sails had to be continually hauled around to take advantage of every breeze. Sails would be taken down here, carefully overhauled and stowed away in the sail locker, and replaced by a second set. Eventually a gentle wind would be felt, indicating that the ship was getting to the other side.

Masters had to use their own experience to navigate. Compasses could be poor quality and unreliable and the Master was supposed to supply his own maps, which could be of limited value, although they generally improved in quality throughout the Century. "Physical Geography of the Sea and its Meteorology' was published in 1864, one of the first more reliable Atlases[34].

The *Ottawa* left Calcutta after only 20 days. By July 18th she was reported off Madagascar and by September 14th was off Gambia on the West coast of Africa, arriving at the Albert Dock in Liverpool on October 16th. She carried a cargo of rice, saltpetre, cotton, jute, rapeseed, cowhides, kidskins, gunny cloth, indigo, and linseed. This is the sort of high quality cargo that only a good ship can carry, as it would be easily damaged if there was any chance she might spring a leak. Unfortunately, it was at this point that she was involved in her first collision.

THE CARRIER DOVE INCIDENT

This episode reads like a sort of slow motion Keystone Cops movie, but because it resulted in court cases we have a great deal of information about it, and it must have been typical of the sort of incident that sailing ships might be involved in (the map perhaps makes it a bit clearer, Figure 3).[35] The *Carrier Dove* was a large American vessel registered in New York, at 1545 tons much bigger than the *City of Ottawa*. She was carrying an expensive cargo of grain and other merchandises, giving a total value for ship, freight and cargo of £35,000. Her Master was John Howell Jackson and her owner, Benjamin John Harriot Trask the Younger of New York, was also on board on his first visit to Liverpool. She arrived there on 15th October 1862, and anchored between the North landing stage and Seacombe, discharging her cargo. She had not completed this exercise by 19th, which was a very stormy day, and in the early evening she dragged her anchor and collided with the *Wisconsin*, another large ship at anchor, causing the latter to lose her mizzenmast, and to bounce onto the *Themis*, a British ship, anchored on the other side of the *Wisconsin*. The *Carrier Dove* had lost her port anchor and chain, so hung blue lights and sent up rockets, to signal that she needed help. This was answered by the *Enterprise* and the *Universe*, which were two of the little paddle steamer tugs that operated up and down the Mersey. At this stage it was 8.00 in the evening, nearly at high tide, with a very heavy sea and strong gale from the South. When the *Enterprise* arrived the two ships, the *Carrier Dove* and *Wisconsin*, were lying locked together, but the *Enterprise* towed the *Carrier Dove* clear, while the *Universe* towed *Wisconsin* to Prince's Basin.

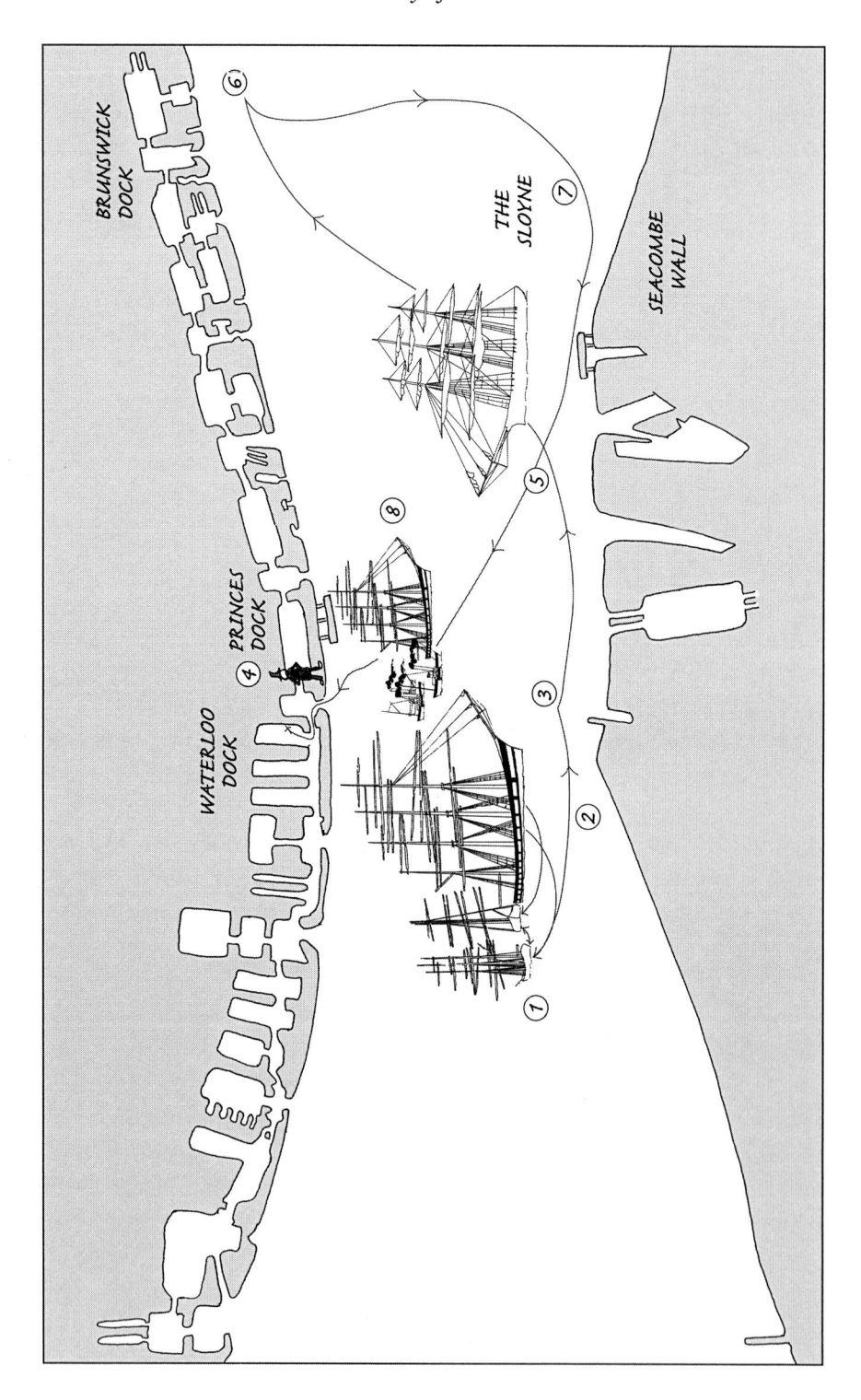

The City of Ottawa

Life of a Ship: First Years

Figure 3 (facing page): Plan of the *Carrier Dove* incident, showing how far the vessel strayed, and also giving some idea of the complexity of the Liverpool Dock system at that time.

1. 19th October 8.00 pm a heavy ebb tide. The *Carrier Dove* slipped its moorings, hit the *Wisconsin*, damaging her, then hit the *Themis*

2. The *Enterprise*, a steam tug, pulled her away but she swung on her moorings and struck the *Themis* twice more.

3. 20th October, 2.30 pm, the *Carrier Dove* was at last anchored safely

4. By 5.00 pm Captain Trask had landed at Prince's Dock

5. 7.00 pm squally flood tide. The *City of Ottawa* was anchored in The Sloyne. The *Carrier Dove* was out of control again, floating upstream dragging the *Enterprise*. She struck the *City of Ottawa*, as the *Enterprise* nipped out of the way of the larger ships

6. The *Carrier Dove* nearly smashed into Brunswick Dock before the *Enterprise* caught her up

7. Now without rudder or anchor, she was held steady by two tugs overnight off Monk's Ferry

8. 21st October 8.00 am, flood tide. The *Carrier Dove* was at last towed backwards into the Waterloo Dock by three tugs, the *Enterprise*, the *Universe* and the *Constitution*

Unfortunately at this stage the wind and tide both changed, and the *Carrier Dove* swung on her moorings, again colliding with the poor *Themis*, which wasn't much damaged. The *Enterprise* once more towed the *Carrier Dove* clear, and held her all night.

The next day the Master of the *Carrier Dove* wanted to haul in her anchor and proceed to a safe anchorage in dock, but when the crew started to heave in the chain, it was found to be inextricably hooked around another one, which turned out to have previously belonged to the *Wisconsin*. This delayed matters so much that it was impossible to dock that tide. It took all day until 4.00 in the afternoon to sort out the anchors, when with the foreign chain slipped and catted, the *Carrier Dove* was towed southwards off the South end of Seacombe wall, where she anchored with her own starboard anchor.

The City of Ottawa

Now relations worsened with the tugs, as Captain Trask, whom we might picture as overconfident, brash even, refused to pay the sums the Captains of the tugs requested and an argument ensued, with the tug Captains eventually agreeing that the amount should be decided by a third party. No doubt the fees were rather high, and perhaps the tug Captains hoped to take advantage of an inexperienced American, but then they had a monopoly on an expert and essential service and Captain Trask might have done well to have paid them. (The court records refer to him as 'Captain', though it is not clear what right he had to the title).

At this point the latter left his ship and went ashore in a small rowing boat to arrange docking. The *Enterprise* went to pick him up at 5.45 from the Prince's landing stage, but was told to wait while he went to Waterloo Dock. Eventually they went back to the ship, but the weather was worsening again, and at the flood tide a heavy squall caused the *Carrier Dove* to slip her anchor and float rapidly downstream towards the *City of Ottawa*, with only the little *Enterprise* trying to hold her.

It seems that by the 20th the *Ottawa* had discharged her cargo and was anchored in the Sloyne, in the channel outside the dock system and about ¼ mile downstream of the *Carrier Dove*, in the charge of a Liverpool Pilot, John Boulter Pryor, as was the custom. She had a bright light hanging on the forestay, a man at the wheel, and crew on sea watch. When the *Carrier Dove* starting driving down the river towards her, she was hailed to put her helm to starboard, which she immediately did, but nevertheless the *Carrier Dove* struck her on her starboard bow which was stove in, while the topgallant forecastle deck was buckled and her bowsprit, shrouds and head-rail knees carried away. The *Enterprise* had been attempting to hold up the *Carrier Dove*, but at this stage she cut the hawser and jumped clear, fearing to be caught between the two much bigger ships. Consequently the *Carrier Dove* canted westwood, carrying away the port anchor stopper of the *Ottawa*, which caused the anchor to run down, unshipping the cathead, and doing other damage.

The *Carrier Dove* then fell across the bows of the *City of Ottawa* and went down her on the port side, when the stern and rudder of the *Carrier Dove* crossed the chain of the *City of Ottawa*. The *Carrier Dove* drifted sternfirst over the river to Brunswick Dock wall, where the *Enterprise* and *Universe* caught her and, turning her head to the ebb tide, towed her to a safe anchorage between Toxteth and Brunswick Docks, heading North by East, about 200 yards from the wall, but because of her bad steering couldn't bring her off head foremost, and instead had to tow her backwards, eventually anchoring off Monk's Ferry with the foreign anchor.

Life of a Ship: First Years

The next day, the 21st October, at 8 a.m., again on a flood tide with a strong wind from the North West, the crew of the *Carrier Dove* at last realised that they had lost their rudder during the collision with the *Ottawa* – it seems rather careless of them not to have noticed it sooner. The ship was towed with difficulty to the South end of the Seacombe wall and with the help of a third tug, the *Constitution*, was towed across the river, eventually docking safely in the Waterloo Dock, to the general relief of all concerned.

We owe our detailed knowledge of the events to the two court cases that followed, Kenneth Dowie claiming a sum in damages for repair of the *Ottawa*, and the three tug captains suing Trask for the fees they claimed. Captain Trask does not come across as a sympathetic character. It was his first visit to Liverpool, and his ignorance of local conditions must have contributed to the accident. His hard headed bargaining and unwillingness to pay the going rate meant that his vessel was not secured by enough tugs to hold her. And despite the fact that it was clearly his fault, he refused to pay for the damage done to the *Ottawa* until forced to do so. On the other hand the incident took place during the American Civil War, when Liverpool as a whole sided with the secessionist South, with whom they had business connections through the cotton and slave trades (although it had been formally abolished in 1807, slavery continued in some Southern States and Africans continued to be deported to America until about 1860. In addition Liverpool had become a major importer of cotton). So there may well have been some prejudice against a captain from New York in the Yankee North, and certainly the £4000 that the tug captains first asked for was considered excessive even by a sympathetic court. Captain Trask initially paid only £170, but eventually the two sides settled for a total of £1075: £600 to the *Enterprise*, £450 to *Universe* and £25 to *Constitution*, but not before the cases went on appeal to the Judicial Committee of Privy Council, which supported the judgement of the lower court (the Court of Admiralty) and found against the American on all counts in April and July 1863 respectively.

Although Captain Jackson was named as Captain of the *Ottawa* he did not give evidence so presumably he was not on board at the time and perhaps had already left for his next vessel. In any case he went on to have a distinguished career. Over the next 4 years he made annual journeys to Calcutta for cotton on board the *Eliza Bencke*, during which according to his daughter Maria he encountered Chinese pirates, a tidal wave, and was stranded on a coral reef[36]. After a year on the *Yumuri*, he took over the *Rooparell* on her maiden voyage to bring back 2023 packages of tea from Calcutta. This was the peak of his career: the iron sailing ship was built for speed as a tea clipper in Glasgow and had the highest Lloyds rating of AA1 21 years. Jackson took her three times to

Calcutta and back over the next three years. She managed some fast speeds: on her maiden voyage she took 135 days out and 83 days back. When he did the journey on the *Ottawa* it took 177 days out and 90 days back, although weather was always a factor of course.

Although the *Rooparell* was built to be speedier than the *Ottawa* she did not have her sailing qualities (and perhaps luck). Her career was varied but short. As she had two decks she was more flexible (and a little larger) than the *Ottawa* and after Jackson left she carried pig iron to New York, 361 immigrants to New Zealand (the largest number hitherto carried at one time), and wool to Australia. But she was declared missing en route to Negapatam in India with coal in 1878 after only 10 years at sea and in that creepy way that sailing ships had she disappeared completely from history except that a year later the barque the *Countess of Derby* arriving in New York from Rio di Janeiro reported that on June 10th off the Abrolbos Islands (off the western coast of Australia) a lifebuoy was found apparently having spent some time in the water with 'Rooparell of Glasgow' painted on it and also a Maltese cross. The *Rooparell* was much heavier than the earlier tea clippers (Lloyds Register notes that she had 'heavier plating than the Rules now require) and experienced difficulties with steering throughout her life.

To return to Jackson, after leaving the *Rooparell* in 1871 he was apparently unemployed for a while, but then in about 1875 went to work for the Beaver Line. This was the nickname of the Canada Steamship Company that ran steamers from Liverpool or London to Montreal, Quebec and New York with emigrants, freight and live cattle. Initially Jackson seems to have commanded the *Lake Winnipeg* then in 1885 took over the *Lake Manitoba* but unfortunately this did not end well. A Reuter's telegram was reported in the Morning Post of 1 July 1885, which said that 'the steamer *Lake Manitoba* which went ashore off St Pierre Miquelon about a fortnight ago has become a total wreck' with a cargo of about 1900 tons and a number of cattle, 54 crew, 9 passengers and 15 drovers on board. She had set off from Montreal for Liverpool at half past six on the morning of June 11 and on arriving at Quebec (further downstream) discharged her river pilot and took on one for the navigation of the Gulf of the St Lawrence. On the 12th he was in turn discharged and shortly after 3 o'clock the next day the vessel passed Cape Ray on the western tip of Newfoundland at a distance of about 4 or 5 miles. While the First Officer slept and with the Second Officer on duty on deck, Captain Jackson was examining his charts in his cabin when the vessel struck on the island of Miquelon, just south of Newfoundland. The Second Officer subsequently claimed that the vessel had just entered a thick fog and although there was a lighthouse and foghorn this did not start to sound till half an hour later. The first three boats were smashed by the surf on being launched but everyone on board escaped safely in five other boats: but the steamer was wrecked and presumably the cattle did not come to a good end either.

By 20th August an enquiry was being held in Liverpool to ascertain blame. Over three days the court considered whether there had been a navigational error. The Second Officer claimed he was following the navigational directions given and blamed 'a sudden unknown current'. The President remarked that sirens requiring steam to be got up seemed to be 'most unsatisfactory and useless things' unless they were worked by machinery day and night as people expected to be able to rely on them. However the fault lay with the Captain in setting a course after Cape Ray that was not made good: i.e. he doesn't seem to have passed on the revised navigational directions. The court said that 'in consideration of his long service, high character and till now uniformly successful career' it would not revoke his certificate (and in fact he subsequently applied for and received a replacement certificate as his previous one went down with the ship). Captain Jackson was now 64 years old. Had he fallen asleep below after the tiring passage from Montreal? The islands of St Pierre and Miquelon were large islands, whose position was well known – not easy to overlook! Anyway he does not seem to have worked again, and died at the good age of 72 in 1893 in Meols, Hoylake, by the shore in the leafy Wirral, a nice place for a Liverpudlian mariner to end his days. He died of cystitis surrounded by his family, so was one of the few Masters who died a non-sailing related death.

The collision of the *City of Ottawa* with the *Carrier Dove* seems to have turned Kenneth Dowie against shipowning, as the vessel was again put up for sale, and was advertised between 28th November and 13th December 1862 in the Liverpool Mercury[37]. The sales advertisement was largely similar to the previous one, but it added, "Her model combines large carrying capacity with good sailing qualities, and she is a very profitable ship. Is well found in stores of every description, and well worthy of inspection. Lying in the Queen's graving dock." This attempt was to be more successful.

---

1   'Québec: les regions de Québec, histoire en bref', Marc Vallières, Les Presses de l'Université Laval 2010

2   'Grandeur et déclin de la construction navale à Québec', Jean Benoît, Cap-aux-Diamants: la revue d'histoire du Québec, no 22, 1990, p 47-50

3   Private communication from Ms Marcil

4   'Rhyl Foryd Harbour. An assessment of the wreck – *City of Ottawa*', Gifford, Report No. 14533 RO1a, December 2007, quoting E. Marcil
5   Shipbuilding Register 1856 – 1865 Vol. 1 E17 1C 018 01-04-001B-02, 1986-10-002/17 Banq
6   "On chantait 'Charley-Man'. La construction de grands voiliers à québec de 1763 à 1893", Eileen Reid Marcil, Les Editions GID, 2000
7   ibid.
8   Lloyds Special Survey, National Maritime Museum
9   'Iron knees in wooden vessels – an attempt at a typology', M Stammers, International Journal of Nautical Archaeology, Vol 30 (1), pp115-121, 2001
10 'Rhyl Foryd Harbour. An assessment of the wreck – *City of Ottawa*', idem
11 Personal communication from E Marcil
12 "On chantait 'Charley-Man'", idem
13 From the classified advertisement of sale in the Liverpool Mercury, Thursday September 27th 1860, The British Newspaper Archive (www.britishnewspaperarchive.co.uk)
14 'The ship. The life and death of the merchant sailing ship 1815 – 1965', Basil Greenhill, Her Majesty's Stationery Office, 1980
15 'The Merchant Sailing Ship: A Photographic History', Basil Greenhill and Ann Giffard, David and Charles, Newton Abbot, 1970
16 "On chantait 'Charley-Man'" idem
17 Lloyds Special Survey, National Maritime Museum
18 Classified advertisement of sale in the Liverpool Mercury Thursday September 27th 1860, The British Newspaper Archive (www.britishnewspaperarchive.co.uk)
19 'The life and times of a merchant sailor. The archaeology and history of the merchant ship Catharine', Jason M Burns, Kluwer Academic/Plenum Publishers, 2003
20 'The ship. The life and death of the merchant sailing ship 1815 – 1965', Basil Greenhill, Her Majesty's Stationery Office, 1980
21 'Liverpool's Historic Waterfront. The world's first mercantile dock system', Nancy Ritchie-Noakes, 1984, HMSO
22 Quebec Morning Chronicle and Commercial and Shipping Gazette, 18th July 1860 and 1st August 1860, Banq database
23 Lloyds Register of Registrations, 1860, Banq
24 Mike Bowyer, Marine Archaeologist, in private communication to the author.
25 Liverpool Mercury, Thursday September 27th, October 2nd & 4th, 1860, The British Newspaper Archive (www.britishnewspaperarchive.co.uk)
26 Customs, Bills of Entry, Liverpool, 1860, Merseyside Maritime Museum
27 Lloyds List Nov 15/Liv6. All references to sailing times have been taken from the relevant edition of the Lloyds List, unless otherwise stated.
28 Lloyds Register of Registrations, 1860, Ref: 280/1861, Merseyside Maritime Museum
29 According to the website www.measuringworth.com. Translating Victorian finances into modern equivalents is not simple as so many factors have changed, but if we look at it in terms of the retail prices index (if there had been such a thing then) we get the former figure, but if we instead consider what the sum tells us about the position of the person in society, we get the latter figure, indicating that Captain Withycombe left quite a tidy sum to his heirs.

30   Wallasey and Wirral Chronicle, October 14 1933, Wirral Archives Service, Birkenhead
31   'The sailing ship – *City of Ottawa*', David Arminas in Argonautica, the newletter of the Canadian Nautical Research Society Vol XXVI, No 1 Jan. 2009
32   'Square – rigged ships: an introduction', Alan Villiers, National Maritime Museum, Greenwich, London, 2009
33   'Reminiscences of a sailor', William R Lord, Historical Collection of the British Library, 1894
34   'Square – rigged ships: an introduction', idem
35   Judicial Committee of Privy Council. Appeal by Benjamin John Harriot Trask the Younger of New York, Owner of Carrier Dove Appellant v. Kenneth McKenzie Dowie merchant of Liverpool, Owner of *City of Ottawa* Appellate, 8th April 1863, *and* BJH Trask and others v Peter Maddox and others, 30th July 1863. Ref: PCAP1/310, National Archives
36   Wallasey and Wirral Chronicle, idem
37   Liverpool Mercury 1862 November 29th et passim, The British Newspaper Archive (www.britishnewspaperarchive.co.uk)

Chapter 2

LIFE OF A SHIP: HEYDAY WITH JOHN BARRETT

1863

The *City of Ottawa* lay in the Queen's graving dock at Liverpool being repaired after the *Carrier Dove* incident, and while she was there she was surveyed and remetalled, which was necessary at frequent intervals to avoid the build up of barnacles etc on her hull. This time she found buyers, Thomas Restarick and Thomas Brown Restarick his son, who acquired her on 22nd January 1863 and transferred her registration to Plymouth[1]. They wasted no time, for by March 30th Thomas Bunker had joined as Mate and the vessel was taking on ballast in Brunswick Dock. On April 2nd she sailed for Quebec, with John Barrett as Master.

John Alfred Barrett was one of the two Masters on the *Ottawa* whose logbooks have survived. He was born in November 1830, in Stoke Damerel, Devonport, Devon to a naval family, and so was aged 33 when he took over the vessel. He never married and stayed with his brother Charles' family when in his home port of Plymouth. Two of his brothers, William and George, followed him into the merchant navy and sometimes sailed with him, and indeed William sailed as an Able Seaman on the first three voyages for which crew lists have survived[2]. More details of John's life can be found in Chapter 7.

On April 4th at 3.00 in the afternoon, the tug *Rattler* spotted the *Ottawa* 15 miles North West of Bardsey Island, the wind at Holyhead being West South West with a fresh gale. She arrived in Quebec on May 14th, and by 29th sailed for Plymouth at the same time as the *Eliza*, mentioned above. On 27th June she reached Plymouth for the first time, doubtless carrying timber. She made two more very rapid passages to Quebec that year, leaving Plymouth after a quick turnaround of three days and arriving in Canada on August 5th, returning to Plymouth on September 6th, only six days after the *Jessie Boyle* which made the quickest second voyage that year. The *Ottawa* arrived in Quebec for the third time around October 11th, well before the St Lawrence froze in November, and was back in Newport by 17th November.

Article from the Freeman's Journal and Daily Commercial Advertiser, which illustrates how much interest there was in such things in those days[3]

Quebec Timber Trade: Plymouth Tuesday. The ship *Jessie Boyle*, Captain W. Symons, which left Quebec on 12th (August), arrived here on Monday the 31st, only two days after the owner's receipt of the Master's sailing letter, which came by mail steamer. The *Jessie Boyle* sailed from Plymouth July 3rd, and has therefore accomplished the voyage out and home in one month and 28 days. Like others, she made a voyage in the spring. Unless the *Shandon* has arrived at Greenock, or the *Jane* at Liverpool, the *Jessie Boyle* is the first ship home to England on the second voyage this year. The *Eliza* and the *City of Ottawa* were left loading. They belong to Plymouth, which has this year despatched nine other ships on their second voyage to Quebec.

The existing crew lists start with the second Restarick voyage, and it seems from this that Barrett achieved these fast speeds partly by retaining seamen over the three voyages to ensure he had an efficient crew, which was quite unusual. To do this he paid bonuses: on the second voyage, the Able Seamen (AB) were receiving £3 a month, by the third this had risen to £3 5s, while the highest rates for Ordinary Seamen (OS) had risen from £2 10s to £2 15s (an 'Able Seaman' was knowledgeable and highly skilled, and probably had at least five years' experience, whereas on 'Ordinary Seaman' was still learning his trade, and was paid according to his abilities and the number of years he had worked. It was quite common for men to come aboard claiming more skill than they actually had, but they were generally weeded out quickly and re-rated). A large proportion of the crew were Plymouth men. In addition to officers (some of whom had previously been on the *Eliza*), seven ordinary seamen stayed over to the second passage, and no less than ten to the third, as well as all the officers and the two apprentices. The concept of moulding the crew into a team was rare among ordinary merchant ships, being mostly confined to the Royal Navy and the higher class Shipping Lines.

A Note on the Second Owners — Thomas Restarick and Thomas Brown Restarick[4]

The story of Thomas Restarick and his son Thomas Brown Restarick is worth looking at in depth as it gives us a great deal of insight into the lives of the small shipowner and the profitability of the business.

Thomas Restarick was born in 1793 in Devonport, married Elizabeth and had five children, three girls, Martha, Elizabeth and Sabina, and two sons John and Thomas. All the children took a second name 'Brown', their mother's maiden name. Thomas Brown Restarick was the youngest, born 1835, and it was he who entered into the family business with his father.

The family grew up in James Street, Devonport, the smart part of Plymouth, and the baptismal registers record Thomas' progress from shipbuilder, to ship's chandler, then merchant. It seems the household was sufficiently well off to employ a servant, and secure good marriages for some at least of the daughters, though there was also always a link to the sea. The eldest, Martha, married the lodger Robert Jackson, Master Mariner, in 1841 and it seems went to live in London, but died before 1861, leaving one son, also Robert, who was living with his grandparents by that year[5]. Next was Elizabeth, who was possibly married twice – first in 1846, but whatever happened to that marriage, in the 1851 and 1861 censuses she was back home, living under her maiden name and calling herself 'unmarried'. However she remarried on 26 April 1865 to John Jeffreys, a moderately wealthy landowner in St Budeaux, Plympton parish, with some seven acres and two employees (all family baptisms and marriages took place at Tamerton Foliott church, their mother's birthplace). The family also comprised a cook and housemaid. At the next census in 1881 John was a Commission Agent, and the household included his elderly unmarried sister, two general servants, and also a governess, Edith Bexford Smith (an unmarried 29 year old) and 5 young wards aged between 9 and 14, from Calcutta. Clearly this was run as a business.

The next son, John, died aged 21 in 1852, and was perhaps always sickly, as he never seems to have had a profession.

Sabina, the next child, was the success story of the family, marrying John Rolston, a surgeon and general practitioner, and proceeding to have nine children with exotic names like Cecilia, Ada, Blanche and Florence. Clearly they were even more well to do, living in Clarendon House, Devonport, and employing three or four servants, including cook, housemaid and childsmaid.

Thomas was the member of the family who inherited his father's interest in ships. He first went to sea in 1854, aged 19, on the *Edward*, one of his father's ships, then in 1855 as supercargo (the officer in charge of cargo and the commercial concerns of the voyage) on the *Princess Royal* which was still in his father's ownership. In 1857 he married Ellen. In 1864 he sailed on the *City of Ottawa* as OS, though only outward to Genoa – possibly to meet trade contacts out there.

Thomas Restarick Senior owned some 19 ships over 32 years, starting in a small way with the *William Henry*, a 19 ton barge which he apparently bought new in 1832 and sold a year later. The *City of Ottawa* was the last ship he bought. Ten of them were built in Canada, in Quebec, or in St John or Portland, New Brunswick. He bought four of them new from Quebec, the *Kalmia, Emperor, Edward* and *Eliza*, all built in the yard of Thomas H Oliver, or later James E Oliver[6]. The biggest vessels he owned were *Princess Royal*, 1109 tons, then *Eliza*, 942 tons, followed by the *City of Ottawa*. His seamen quite often switched between these ships and the *Countess of Loudon*, next largest at 785 tons, and in the early 1860s the *Ottawa* and *Eliza* often sailed between Quebec and Plymouth at the same time. Five of his ships were lost or abandoned, the rest were sold – the most he owned at any one time was seven during most of 1856. We get the impression he made a good living out of them. Two of them, the *Countess of Loudon* and the *City of Ottawa*, were owned jointly with his son.

At his death on 13th October 1864 some three remained, which were taken over by Thomas Junior. They were the three biggest vessels, mentioned above. Of these the *Princess Royal* was lost in the St Lawrence on 8th September 1869 and the *Eliza* similarly in the Newfoundland fogs at Cape Breton on 4th June 1871, at which point the *Ottawa* was mortgaged. So the *Ottawa* was his only remaining ship when she was sold to John Porter Rogers on 19th July 1873, and we get the idea he was struggling financially. He then apparently went back to sea as an AB and died in 1878 at the age of 43 on board the *Jessie Readman* of dropsy, probably the result of kidney failure[7]. No pay was owing, as he was in debt to the ship.

As we will see, the *Ottawa*'s next owner, John Porter Rogers, also struggled financially as time went on and we have to conclude that shipowning was always an uncertain profession, especially as the century progressed, subject to sudden, random losses and frequent cash flow problems.

1864–5

However, back in 1864, the *Ottawa* overwintered in Newport, in the newly enlarged Town Dock, and probably loaded up with coal – Newport, like Cardiff, was benefiting from the world demand for the high grade bituminous variety from the Gwent Valley. It was preferable to sail in warmer seas during the winter, so the vessel set off again on 24th January, this time for Genoa, arriving 25th February. Wages for ABs had dropped to £2 17s 6d and Barrett's crack team of seamen dispersed: only officers and apprentices stayed on this time, although the crew still included William, John's brother. William was the younger by 10 years and it seems he went to sea at the age of 20 as an unmarried Ordinary Seaman on board the *Eliza Ann*, then to the *Startled Fawn* before joining the *Ottawa*. Also on the crew list this time were William Dunn, later to be Master of the *Ottawa*, as AB, and Thomas Brown Restarick, who was then joint owner with his father, as mentioned above. The *Ottawa* stayed in Genoa until 14th April, perhaps seeking a cargo, but when she sailed Barrett unwillingly left behind one of the apprentices, Henry Tiltman, on the insistence of the doctor of the hospital. Although only 17 he had venereal disease. He was on his third passage on the *Ottawa*, and the third year of his indenture, and came from a good maritime background, as his father was Chief Boatman at the Coast Guard Station at Downderry St Germans. Nevertheless it seems he went on to make full recovery, married in 1876 at the age of 29, and after a career in the Royal Navy (he was Quarter Master in 1881) settled down in Downderry St Germans, Cornwall, to have 2 sons and enjoy a long married life. He became a coastguard like his father and was mentioned in the Western Daily Press of 2nd September 1887 as being involved in a coastguard rescue at Seaton. On his death at the age of 73 of cerebral thrombosis and cancer of the tongue he left £370 (worth today £13,600, or £75,400 by the same measure as that used for Withycombe's inheritance) to his heirs – for a fuller discussion of the medical implications see Chapter 10.

The *Ottawa* sailed in ballast to Quebec again, but an Italian stowaway in the hold was quickly discovered. It would be relatively easy to sneak in there while the crew were eating or otherwise engaged, but it could be a dangerous place to be after the ship set sail. On this occasion the ship was in ballast and the Italian made an appearance a day out of port, but he apparently had no papers and did not speak English, so Captain Barrett didn't manage to find out his name, or any information about him. Unfortunately on 8th May just after midday he contrived to fall overboard when he overbalanced while drawing a bucket of water. Seamen who fell into the sea were very lucky if they were rescued, as they could hardly ever swim, and of course a sailing ship has no brakes, and is slow to respond to changes of direction. In addition it is almost impossible to tell looking back exactly where someone fell into the water. On this occasion, although the helm was put about immediately and the Quarter Boat lowered, he could not be found. Captain Barrett speculated that 'he disappeared in about 2 minutes after his falling and I think he must of got entangled in the bucket rope'. He had no effects on board and could not be identified so there seemed to be nothing more to be done.

The *Ottawa* arrived in Quebec on June 5th, safely after the thaw and when there was no longer danger of icebergs. She came back to Plymouth on July 19th with a cargo of timber. By July 28th she was off again, arriving at Quebec on 2nd September, and setting off for home on 16th. As she sailed back up the St Lawrence towards the open sea, it was noted in the Lloyds List that there were several icebergs in the channel already. She was back in Plymouth on October 17th. This was far too late to try to get to Quebec again that year so on December 10th she sailed for Malaga. In the meantime the title passed solely to Thomas Brown Restarick as his father had died. The vessel arrived at Malaga on 27th December, having spent Christmas at sea, and got back to Plymouth on 19th February next year. In that year, 1865, she again managed to fit in three passages Plymouth to Quebec, with a very quick turnaround in each port, leaving finally on November 2nd, at great risk of icebergs. She arrived in Plymouth on 25th November, then in December sailed for Newport, overwintering in Penarth for her usual winter period survey and repairs. No crew lists or log books have survived for these five passages but we know that Barrett remained Master.

A Note on Plymouth

The *City of Ottawa* was registered to Plymouth for most of her working life, and the port played a big part in her story. Three of her Masters (Barrett, Pinhey, Dunn) and two of her owners (Thomas Restarick and Thomas Brown Restarick) came from there, and it was often her British port of destination.

Plymouth originally comprised three townships, Devonport, Stonehouses and Plymouth itself. The elegant naval barracks were finished in 1785, but this was followed by improvements to the merchant port also, with construction of a breakwater across the Sound by 1841, which provided one of largest sheltered anchorages in Europe, better facilities at Sutton Pool including a railway link, and, by 1870, the opening of the Great Western Docks at Millbay, effectively a second harbour with deep docking facilities. By mid-century, the three towns had become Devon's biggest urban centre which attracted people in from the whole area (for instance, Captain Dunn, and his friend Thomas Showan, as we will see) and led to an economy based mainly on maritime activities, including commercial shipbuilding and repairing, mercantile trade and broking and import based manufacturing industries, as well as the army and navy[8].

While the London architect John Foulston was designing elegant terraces and spacious squares of stuccoed houses for middle class families, where Thomas Restarick and John Barrett's brother Charles lived, there was still a considerable area of poor overcrowded old insalubrious housing around the Sutton Pool: this was where Captain Henry Pinhey was brought up. And in 1871, 1,080 paupers resided in Plymouth workhouse, of which Thomas Showan's 9 year-old sister Elizabeth was one.

1866–7

The *Ottawa*'s next voyage was much longer, as she sailed to Bombay (now Mumbai), still with Barrett as Master and Bunker as Mate and this time John's youngest brother George, aged 19, as one of the five apprentices. George Barrett was born in 1848, the baby of the family, and 17 years younger than John who was already at sea when he was born. After his parents' death he lived at the house of his sister Elizabeth and was indentured at the age of 14. All the officers apart from the cook had also been on previous voyages. Wages were low, at £2 15s a month for an AB, and Captain Barrett had problems getting a full complement of 20 men plus apprentices. Coming from Plymouth in December, he signed on the crew at Newport, but two did not turn up and another deserted. Sailing on to Penarth at the beginning of March to load coal, an AB was discharged as he had been offered the position of Mate on another ship, two more deserted, and two of those signed up as replacements never arrived either. The final two were shipped while the boat was in the lock, cleared to sail, and the rushed nature of the transaction is shown by the fact that their signature on the Ship's Articles was witnessed by G E Smith, the porter at the Sailor's House.

The *Ottawa* arrived in Bombay on June 14th. The log records proudly that two days later the Master took his brother, now out of his apprenticeship, before the Shipping Master to sign his articles as an AB. In Bombay he picked up a very good cargo comprising 2954 bales of cotton, 985 bales of wool, one bundle of bamboos, 359 bags of linseed, 200 bales coir yarn, 3 cases of 'Japan works' and 2 boxes of bison head and horns – presumably hunting trophies[9]? These all filled orders by different merchants and agents, and show how various commissions would be picked up until the hold was full and the ship could leave.

The ship sailed on October 2nd and was nearly back in home waters when there was a tragic incident: on 13th January 1867 while the vessel was off the coast of Spain William Nuttle the Boson died of consumption. He had first fallen ill in Bombay – for more discussion of the medical implications see Chapter 10. A Plymouth man, he had sailed on every voyage to this point for which records remain, and presumably the five in the middle for which they do not, so his loss must have been deeply felt. He had been married at the age of 20 to Sarah Ann, and had four children: his eldest, Sarah, died when she was 10, but at least three survived, William, 14, Harry, 4, or Clara, only 1 year old at his death, all living in Hooe, near Plymouth. He was a provident man, as shown by the list of his possessions (see Chapter 8) which included spices and chutneys and a sewing kit. He was buried immediately at sea and his property sold to the rest of the crew for a total of £22 4s 10d, which added to his backpay made a total of £35 1s 2d, quite a good sum to be handed to his next of kin.

Just before the vessel arrived at Liverpool on 25th January John Berry Arnold, apprentice, was also made up to AB – the voyage had lasted just under a year. It had been completed in the fast time of 100 days out and 115 days back, which indicates what a good ship the vessel was in her prime, though wind and weather were always a factor of course.

From February 1st to March 1st 1867 the vessel was taking on cargo in the Queens Dock, Liverpool for P Sutherland and G Warren and Co. Several vessels were loading goods destined for Boston on behalf of the latter company at the same time, and it is unfortunately impossible to distinguish which cargo was intended particularly for the *Ottawa*, but it seems she was delayed until it arrived and was passed by Customs. At the same time the vessel had her annual survey and she sailed on March 3rd, all repairs satisfactorily carried out. Perhaps because they were heading for Boston, wages were a little higher this time, at £3 5s, but only two apprentices remained on the ship's articles. Russell Giddy took over as Bosun, and Joseph Chilcott, who had sailed the previous eight voyages as Carpenter's Mate, was made up to Carpenter.

The *Ottawa* sailed into Boston on April 15th, and the Lloyds List reports that she arrived 'disabled', although this is not mentioned in the log book.

Whether because of this or because of the attractions of a big wealthy exciting city, eight men deserted while they were there. Four ABs were also taken on at Boston, at the higher rate of £4 10s, which perhaps explains why some had found it tempting to desert. These men received a balance of pay at the end of the voyage as high or higher than the crew who had worked the entire passage, which must have been annoying to the latter. The day after sailing the apprentice Thomas Symonds Angear was made up to Bosun's Mate, and two days later two stowaways were found: 'John Carney and Frederick Gartland having come to sea in this ship from Boston without anyone's permission put them on the articles to be discharged at Quebec by their own consent'. One was described as OS and the other as 'landsman', but no doubt they helped to make up the numbers. They were put down in the Ship's Articles to receive wages at £2 a month, and were set down at Quebec, after 15 days sailing, with 6.26Ca$, or approximately 18s 6d in their pocket, which seems quite generous[10]. At Quebec two more deserted, one of whom was Edward Hay Archer (perhaps feeling lonely as the only remaining apprentice) and one man was discharged. Although this left crew numbers relatively low at 20, only one man was taken on, quite likely because he received the going rate of £8 a month which shows how high wages were in Quebec.

The vessel took on her usual cargo of wood in two weeks, and sailed for Plymouth, arriving July 14th. She went across to Cardiff, where she loaded (almost certainly with coal) for St Vincent on the Cape Verde Islands, and John Barrett's brother William sailed as Bosun's Mate this time (George had temporarily left to sail on the Restarick vessel *Princess Royal*). When the vessel returned to Cardiff 'Charles Meyer AB fell against the bulwarks and dislocated his wrist', so the Master 'put it in again and bandaged it as well as it could be done on board.' On arriving on November 16th three crewmembers went absent without leave, and Barrett deducted two days' pay from each. They were required to help unload.

After reloading with coal, the vessel sailed on December 12th, anchoring in the Penarth Roads on the 13th to take on crew, and sailing on 18th. Peter Kirby, who signed up right on the last minute, apparently managed to negotiate a higher wage as a consequence, as he received £2 12s 6d a month, which was 2s 6d more than the other ABs. The *Ottawa* was still held up by strong winds, prevalently from the North West, and it was only on 20th December that these changed to South Easterlies, which enabled to ship to get underway. Consequently by the 21st, the vessel was still off Lundy Island where the Master tested the skills of the crew but found John Johnson, who claimed to be an AB 'could not steer' and as he knew very little about the ship, he was demoted to 'a poor O Seaman'. Likewise with the strangely named Groomin Petrosich from Trieste who knew nothing about the compass or steering the ship. The Captain evidently called the men to the wheel in turn, and if they did not know how to steer, questioned them further to ascertain what pay they were worth.

A Note on Communications

The parameters of a voyage had to be set out in detail in the Ship's Articles. Those for the passage of 1867 – 9 illustrate how comprehensive they could be: 'From Cardiff to Aden and/or any other port or ports in the East Indies, China, China Seas, Mediterranean or in any direction freight may offer and back to a final port of discharge in United Kingdom or Continent of Europe calling for orders if required, voyage not to exceed two years.'[11]

The preparation of the Captain's instructions required much thought, and every contingency had to be prepared for, as up to this time there had been no cables to send subsequent instructions. Finding cargos at foreign ports were uncertain and could be very competitive, and sometimes provision had to be made to load or unload ballast. But the most carefully worded instructions could not provide for everything, and often the Captain did something stupid.[12]

Radio signals were not harnessed until 1895 by Marconi, but the system of sending Morse Code messages through telegraph wires was developed throughout the 19th Century. In 1851 a functional telegraph cable had been laid across the English Channel, and by 1866 Cyrus Field managed to lay two cables across the Atlantic to Newfoundland. Over the next years, underwater cables linked the Middle East with India, and Singapore with Australia, and by the end of the century a lot of the world was connected. So from that date onwards, the Master of the *Ottawa* would have been in increasingly better contact with the owners wherever the ship travelled.

1868–9

The *Ottawa* had been at sea for three months before Captain Barrett discovered that Matthew Madden was not up to scratch: 'having relieved John Nelson AB at the wheel the ship at the time being under close reefed top sails whole foresail fore top mast mizzen stay sails and storm spanker the wind being south course NE by E he had not been to the wheel more than 20 minutes before he had the ship from E by N to N by E when told of his bad steering became very abusive sent him from the wheel when he was relieved by Thomas Manning AB who steered within ½ point each way with a little care'[13]. They were sailing speedily northwards up the East coast of Africa towards Aden with a great deal of sail ('stay sails' were extra sails added to the stays to give more speed). They arrived at Aden on 19th May 1868 (it would be with a cargo of coal for the steamers which refuelled there), and the French Consul intervened in the case of Victor Dubro from Lorraine who was in and out of hospital with chest pains. The Consul arranged for him to be sent home.

They sailed on for Moulmein (now Mawlamyine), Burma, on June 29th, arriving on 31st July. Here Matthew Madden who had been bad tempered at the wheel wanted to leave, and Barrett 'took him before the Shipping Master and discharged him'. In Moulmein they must have picked up a cargo for France, as they sailed for Toulon on September 17th, after quite a long delay. However while still off Senegal off the west coast of Africa, on January 7th 1869, a deputation of six seamen went to John Barrett complaining that the beef was 'stinking and they could not eat it'. Barrett promised to open another tierce (or barrel), but two days later (as beef and pork were served on alternate days) three seamen came again on behalf of the whole crew, saying that the beef from the new tierce was no better. So Barrett 'served out a full allowance of pork in its place and kept the beef for inspection when getting into port'. Presumably they managed to make do with this until they put into Cadiz on February 13th. It is hardly surprising that the meat was going off when we consider that it had perhaps been taken on in Cardiff over a year previously, then been carried round hot countries with no refrigeration. It is a miracle the pork was any better. Or the Captain may have picked up poor quality meat in Burma. When they arrived on March 11th at Toulon, John Barrett left the *Ottawa*, never to return.

A Note on Food

From the Merchant Seaman's Act of 1850, the amount of food and drink issued was regulated in the Ship's Articles, and remained fairly consistent throughout the period. Below is given the scale for 1863. The diet actually provides for a lot of meat, equivalent to a very large steak daily, although this would be salted to preserve it, and as we have seen was far from fresh by the end of the voyage. 1lb of bread is the weight of a small modern loaf, but would be in the form of dry ship's biscuit, dry and heavy. Approximately 1 oz of tea per week comprises roughly one fifth of a packet, and crew received about a small jar of coffee, and half a packet of sugar over the same period. The only vegetable provided initially was dried peas, so seamen were eating a lot of carbohydrate and protein (which they needed to support their active lifestyle) but very little fruit or vegetables. From 1867 lime or lemon juice in sugar or rum were to be served daily to prevent scurvy, and this went some small way to rectify this. Old photographs show that seamen were never fat (apart from some Masters!). Maria Williams, daughter of Captain Jackson mentioned above, recounted how "Long before we reached the Indian Ocean our fresh provisions were exhausted: the potatoes were all demolished long ago and the butter had turned nasty and bad, so that we preferred to go without it. Our livestock was gradually getting less but we had two good pigs on board which had a litter of fourteen little pigs. How we enjoyed suckling pig for dinner!"

From 1870 the scale was modified to allow cocoa or chocolate to be substituted for tea, molasses for sugar, and rice, potatoes, yams or barley to be substituted for the flour and peas, but without in general increasing the total amount overall. In 1873 butter could be used to replace some of the beef or pork, and from 1882, there is provision for soup, tinned meat, preserved or compressed vegetables, so the sailor's diet was being gradually improved by new methods of processing food. The Ship's Articles generally stated that there was to be no grog or spirits allowed on board, which might explain why some crew members got regularly blotto when in port, although the Master's discretionary brandy is mentioned below.

Carrying enough fresh water was a problem, and three quarts is not a lot in a hot climate, when washing self and clothes might have to be sacrificed. Clearly some thrived on the diet: the steward John Willcocks sailed for forty years, without apparently suffering more than minor ailments. Of course crew were able to purchase extra supplies when in port, and William Lord recounts going on shore in Spain on a Sunday with his friends, to buy a basket of fruit[14], so not everyone spent all their money on women and drink. Nuttle, the Bosun who died of consumption, had two pieces of ginger, three bottles of chutney, seven bottles of chillies and two bottles of pepper in his sea chest, which must have helped to disguise the flavour of the salt beef and pork. Ships often carried live hens and pigs, which travelled in cages lashed to the deck, to provide fresh meat and eggs. Some Masters provided decent food, replenished when the ship went into port[15], and, perhaps because of incidents of sickness, the conscientious Pinhey notes in the Log that on 27th November 1872 (while still in the Bay of Bengal) he served lime juice and next day 'From leaving port up to this day preserved meats and either potatoes or yams served to crew also fruit once a week all extra in lieu of nothing, also currants in rice Saturday'. After a long journey, the

Master might be hoping to survive on stocks without replenishing supplies, as was the case of John Barrett, above. The six day journey from Le Havre to Plymouth in 1880 did not warrant restocking, and it was specified that the existing supplies of food would be 'sufficient without waste'.

Also, clearly, a lot depended on the ability of the cook. Quite often the offices of cook and steward were combined, especially towards the end of the *Ottawa*'s working life, and some cooks were quite elderly, although most were younger men. There was very little continuity in cooks: sometimes a man would sail for two voyages, but only Richard Slade sailed for three, with Dunn in 1875/6. In fact in 1871, the ship sailed without a cook, as he had failed to join, and managed without one for six days before one could be obtained. Nevertheless, he was not ideal, as it turned out he had venereal disease, and when he was incapacitated one of the ordinary crew members took over, with what success it is not recorded. Again in 1873, the cook John Betty died soon after setting out, and the ship managed for two months before another could be taken on at Pensacola. Griffin sailed two voyages without any cook at all. Pay was generally the lowest of all the ship's officers, only just above the rate paid the men: for instance in 1870 Richard Barrett was paid £3 a month, while ABs were paid £2 12s 6d. All this implies that it was not a highly valued office.

The irritations of the job are shown in the case of John Woods, the cook who sailed for two voyages in 1874, but on the second he got so annoyed because the officers had kept him for too long from his dinner (by lingering over their meal, presumably) that he came aft and swore at them.

	bread	beef	pork	flour	peas	tea	coffee	sugar	water
	lb	lb	lb	lb	pint	oz	oz	oz	qts
Sunday	1	1½		½		1/8	½	2	3
Monday	1		1¼		1/3	1/8	½	2	3
Tuesday	1	1½		½		1/8	½	2	3
Wednesday	1		1¼		1/3	1/8	½	2	3
Thursday	1	1½		½		1/8	½	2	3
Friday	1		1¼		1/3	1/8	½	2	3
Saturday	1	1½				1/8	½	2	3
	One pound butter weekly								

Figure 4: Scale of provisions to be allowed and served out to the crew during the voyage

The City of Ottawa

Did John Barrett leave the *City of Ottawa* because of the problem with the food? Or did he just decide it was time for a change? As Master, Barrett had kept the ship to a quick timetable, with very short stays in port to load and unload, and quick sailing times – we saw above that he was willing to put on a lot of sail if necessary to achieve this. He was ready to pay bonuses to keep on a good crew, and there was a lot of continuity amongst his officers also which implies he inspired a certain loyalty despite having something of a ruthless streak (as shown by the rotten stores he carried). The *Ottawa*, still a good, newish ship, must have been at its most profitable during his period. At a time when ships were out of contact with home and Masters had a lot of autonomy in deciding on destinations, and when there, on finding their own cargos, he had by and large been successful. Details of the rest of his career can be found in Chapter 7.

---

1 Lloyds Register of Registrations, 1863, Plymouth and West Devon Record Office

2 The second crew list calls him 'William Barrett 25 of Cork' but this is surely a mistake as that William Barrett had deserted on the previous voyage

3 Freeman's Journal and Daily Commercial Advertiser, September 4th 1863, The British Newspaper Archive (www.britishnewspaperarchive.co.uk)

4 'Plymouth's other fleet – The Merchant Shipping Registers of the Port of Plymouth', unpublished CD by Gareth E. Hicks.

5 Genealogical details from the appropriate Census forms or Certificates of births, marriages and deaths, available online

6 "On chantait 'Charley-Man'. La construction de grands voiliers à québec de 1763 à 1893", Eileen Reid Marcil, Les Editions GID, 2000

7 Personal communication from Dr Tim Carter, Norwegian Centre for Maritime Medicine, University of Bergen, Norway,

8 'Plymouth's past: so worthy and peerless a western port', Mark Brayshay, in 'Plymouth. Maritime City in Transition', Ed Brian Chalkley, David Dunkerley, Peter Gripaios, Polytechnic South West 1991

9 Customs, Bills of Entry, Liverpool, 1866, Merseyside Maritime Museum

10 Converted using the current exchange rate, according to www.MeasuringWorth.com

11 Crew List, 1867 – 69, Devon Record Office, Exeter

12 'Reminiscences of a Liverpool Shipowner, 1850 – 1920', William Bower Forwood, General Books, originally published 1920. Note the slightly critical attitude he has to Captains!

13 The existing log books and crew lists can be found at the Devon Heritage Centre, ref: 1976/ *City of Ottawa*/36640

14 'Reminiscences of a sailor', idem

15 'Poor Jack. The perilous history of the merchant seaman', Ronald Hope, Chatham Publishing, London 2001

Chapter 3

LIFE OF A SHIP: CRIMPS AND COLLISIONS

1869 CONTINUED

On the departure of John Barrett, Henry Pinhey came to Toulon to take over as Master. He had also been born in Plymouth, on 14th April 1834, and was thus four years younger than Barrett, but while Barrett came from a family closely linked to the sea, Pinhey does not seem to have that connection as his father was a grocer. Nevertheless he encouraged the maritime careers of his two half brothers, Frederick Thomas, born 20th February 1846, and Frank Albert, born 9th February 1853, who both sailed with him from time to time. He had had quite a dashing fast track early career before taking a year off to look after his dying wife - more details of his life can be found in Chapter 7.

William Bunker, the Mate, had also left the *Ottawa* in France, to return home to take his Master's Certificate. All the officers, many of whom had travelled on several voyages with Barrett, left also, with the exception of William Barrett who was now promoted to Bosun. The vessel sailed from Toulon on April 23rd, having taken on a very international crew, comprising six Irish, three Englishmen, three Italians, two West Indians, and one each from the USA, Canada, Scotland, Germany, Gibraltar, Uruguay, Denmark, Netherlands and Africa. Pinhey always seemed to have discipline problems and this passage was no exception, though with all those different languages represented communication may have been difficult. The first incident occurred on May 10th, when he found one Thomas Gill 'whose work was aloft at the time, on the poop with canvas in his possession which had been cut from a bolt there to dry'. Pinhey accused him of cutting it, to which he retorted 'you did not see me do it', which makes him sound rather guilty to me!

When the *Ottawa* arrived at Gibraltar on 23rd May, Pinhey took on two 'working passengers' who wanted to work their way back home, which was an arrangement that he seemed happy to enter into. The Ship's Articles do not record whether they paid him additionally for their keep. George Brown from New York, and Nicholas Krough from St Johns, Newfoundland were put on the ship's articles at the nominal sum of 1s a month, on the understanding they were to be discharged at Quebec, which they duly were with 'no wages due'.

The vessel arrived in Quebec on July 4th, a voyage from Toulon of some 2½ months, and three men promptly deserted. The next day while Pinhey was taking two men to the hospital, three more deserted including Thomas Gill, though whether he took his canvas with him is not recorded. The same day there was an incident involving the Mate, who was an Irishman called James Lawler, a 22 year-old Irishman (who did not handle the crew as well as Bunker) and John Lawrence, the Steward. The latter was 'impertinent to the Mate told him myself to be quiet but he would not calling Mate son of B-h which caused a mush between the two'. When the Captain intervened one James Laughlin ran up drunk, threatening and abusive to join the fray, but the Captain pushed him smartly into the fo'c's'le. Two days later John Lawrence the Steward was again causing trouble: he returned on board, drunk again, threatening to desert, and when the Mate prevented him, 'he took a bayonet from the rack flourished it about and said he would have them, seeing which I shoved [sic] and being afraid of being cut the Mate shoved him down held him and took bayonet from him the steward being much in liquor at the time at last went to his bed'. This is interesting, not only because Pinhey seems to decide it is better to play down his own part in the incident, but also because of the evidence that guns were carried on board, even on a merchant ship, because of the dangers of pirates. After a while the steward was persuaded to go to his quarters and sleep off the alcohol, but he continued to get drunk and neglect his duty for the rest of the stay there. At the same time, men kept slipping off board and staying out without leave, including James Laughlin, the one who had already butted into the fight between the Steward and the Mate.

Danger of Pirates

In some areas there was a real danger of attack, and the crew had to be able to protect the ship. Some ships, mostly American ones, were painted with distinctive white naval markings so that it looked as though they carried cannon. Maria, daughter of Captain Jackson, in her vivid decription of pirates attacking the *Eliza Bencke,* mentions that there were 'a few good rifles' on board, plus revolvers, cutlasses and a big gun that stood on the poop deck. Broken bottles were spread over the deck, as the pirates had bare feet, while the sailors wore good boots.

The wages of the men taken on at Toulon were low, at £2 10s a month, but Pinhey signed on another five in Quebec to replace the six deserters, and had to pay the rate of £10 a month. The port was in the grip of crimps at this time – more on this subject in Chapter 9 – and they tended to push up wage rates, which made deserting more attractive. But this was not quite as advantageous as it seemed as it included an advance of £5, payable to the crimp on completion of the journey. Nevertheless, sailors who took advantage of this still ended up with a balance of over £5 for a month's work whereas the men who served for the entire journey of nearly four months came home with between £2 0s 1½d (in the case of James Laughlin) and £8 13s 8d.

The *Ottawa* left Quebec after twelve incident-packed days for Falmouth, where Bunker rejoined the vessel, still as Mate, although he had now passed his Master's examination. William Bunker sailed for longer than any other crewmember on board the *City of Ottawa*, except for John Willcocks, the steward. He had already sailed with Barrett on other vessels before joining her at the same time in 1863 when she was bought by Restarick, and he sailed as Mate on at least 14 voyages over 11 years, having, we feel, a close friendly relationship with both Barrett and Pinhey. He must have been a popular man and a good Mate, as he is never mentioned in the log books as having problems with the crew, as later Mates sometimes were. He was Irish, from Boyle, County Roscommon, but later described himself as from Plymouth – it was probably easier to find work. More details of his life can be found in Chapter 7.

A Note on the Ship's Officers

The Mate was the chief officer on board ship, second only to the Master. Although the Master was in charge of navigation and manoeuvres, the Mate looked after much of the day-to-day running of the ship, while the Bosun was responsible for rigging and materials. Some Masters gave their Mates an excellent training in navigation and many went on to take their Master's Certificates and get their own command (for instance George Griffin, below), but although William Bunker gained his qualifications, it seems he only once or twice sailed as Master. Perhaps he was more comfortable in the subordinate role.

Most ships also sailed with a carpenter, sailmaker and cook. Of these, the carpenter was the most highly skilled, valued and paid after the Mate – he had an essential role at sea as he was often called upon to carry out repairs after the various accidents that were liable to occur.

The *Ottawa* sailed from Falmouth for Quebec again after only eleven days: Pinhey generally ensured that the unloading process was carried out quickly. This time both Barrett brothers were present, George as Bosun's Mate and William as Bosun, which implies that John Barrett and Henry Pinhey were friends – they were after all near contemporaries and both from Plymouth. In addition, Henry Pinhey's youngest brother Frank, aged 16, joined as 'boy' on his first ship, for pay of 15s a month: the seamen were paid £3 5s each. One William Curnoe was troublesome on the way over as he claimed to have a bad arm so that he could only do light work, but the Master suspected him of malingering.

The *Ottawa* arrived in Quebec on 16th October and while mooring Samuel Gill fell from the mizzen topmasthead whilst sending down the topgallant yard. Although he only bruised himself, he was somewhat shaken, so the Master sent him to bed. No-one deserted due to the lateness of the season, but the loading process was hampered by a small group of men who were persistently misbehaving, going ashore without leave and coming aboard drunk, so that labourers had to be employed in their place. It was important to get the ship ready to leave quickly before the St Lawrence froze in November. Matters continued in this way until 31st October, when the ship was finally ready to sail. On that day, Pinhey called William Curnoe (who was continuing to be troublesome) aft and asked him what was the matter? To which Curnoe replied that he had the horrors. He was shaking badly and Captain Pinhey gave him a glass of brandy. Perhaps it wasn't only the amount of alcohol that William Curnoe had consumed, but also the quality of it.

They had managed to load a cargo of timber in fourteen days but by November 3rd were still navigating the St Lawrence river, the channel linking Quebec to the sea, when the *Ottawa* had a collision with an unlit barque off The Pillars in the middle of the night. This is how Captain Pinhey described it in the log (the reader will have noticed that he wasn't great on punctuation):

'Wind Westerly fresh wind. At 1 a.m. got ship underweigh from Goose Island in charge of branch pilot no[sic] called[sic] and proceeded on our voyage under fore and main topsail foresail and main top gallant sail wind nearly right aft passed several vessels at anchor.'

Life of a Ship: Crimps and Collisions

At 2.30 a.m. a light was reported on the starboard bow. At that point all hands were forward, raising the anchor, a long labour-intensive job, apart from the man who was taking depth soundings, the man at the wheel, the pilot and Captain Pinhey himself, who were on the poop deck. As all seemed to be going well, Captain Pinhey went below into his cabin to 'wipe the compass' (i.e. reset it),

> 'when to my surprise at about 2.40 I heard the chief mate call out hard starboard when I flew out of the cabin the helm was starboarded but ship did not answer quick enough and about 2.45 we collided with a barque at anchor laying tide rode to the flood tide [i.e. swinging in the tide] the same which had been reported before on the starboard bow. The Pilot was steering the vessel by the soundings he received [in margin: 'about a mile west of Pillars'] we struck the vessel in the stern doing what damage I am not aware, the light may have been shut in by his Master the vessel laying tide rode. We commenced shortening sail as soon as clear and cleared away the wreck our foreyard gone in two in the slings gear hanging all foul and anchor not ready so [sic] thought it best to run on until clear proceeded through the Traverses and brought up at 11.30 at the Brandy Pots sent down the foreyard and commenced to scathe it [i.e. to scarph it, or join in a scarph joint] wind WSW strong took in the gig on deck which was smashed.'

Steering a sailing ship is not like steering a car. When the wheel is put over to starboard, the ship takes an appreciable length of time to respond, and in order to steer a straight course, the wheel has to be already put over to port before the ship has completed her turn to starboard. In a strong wind the ship can easily be blown to one side, and it seems the light on the other ship was blown out, or obscured, so the pilot did not see her. The mouth of the St Lawrence was renowned for being an area of mists and fogs, especially so late in the year. Pilots, who were supposed to have expert knowledge of the area, were usually engaged to steer a vessel out of a port, but this was the second time the *Ottawa* was involved in a collision while under the authority of one. It is also interesting that the *Ottawa* continued on her way without finding out if the other ship was damaged (a sailing ship has no brakes! but Captain Pinhey does seem to have had a conscience about this). The *Ottawa* suffered damage to the foreyard (it seems the beam carrying the large front sail was broken in two) and the gig (probably the Pilot's vessel, in tow) although the accident was not entered in the Quebec Lloyds Agency Record Book[1]. The crew included a carpenter and sail maker who were capable of carrying out repairs while at sea, sufficient to sail her home, and she also had further work done on arriving in Cardiff. The vessel did not get back there until December 14th, which indicates a rather longer passage than usual, so perhaps she was held up while the sail was repaired, especially as the wind was largely behind her.

Unfortunately the *Ottawa's* problems that voyage were not finished, as on entering Cardiff Dock on December 14th, she was grounded – a lot of other vessels were damaged at that time in bad weather - although she was got off the next day at high tide.

1870

The *Ottawa's* next Special Survey, to review her rating, was well overdue and could be no longer avoided. She had been sailing for ten years, which was considered the life expectancy of the average wooden sailing ship and she was showing her age. The various bumps and collisions she had experienced had taken their toll and she was not as reliable as she had been. This was carried out while she over-wintered in Cardiff at the same time as her usual survey and maintenance. It was actually rather late as she was originally rated A1 7. According to the Lloyds Register[2], this time she received only an A1 5 rating, which meant that she was beginning to deteriorate and was considered to need reclassification in five years. At the same time she had a major overhaul and was resheathed with Welsh felt and yellow metal.

A Note on Cardiff

A large part of the *Ottawa's* working life was spent in the South Wales coal trade. Cargos are not always recorded, but were almost certain to be coal, as this was really the only thing Cardiff exported. Sometimes the cargo can be identified: 1140 tons of coal in 1874, 1260 tons of coal in 1878 and 1380 tons of coal and sundries in 1869 are noted. Destinations include Bombay, Quebec, Cape Verde, Aden, Rio di Janeiro, and Panama, and exports to the latter four would be for bunkering steam vessels.

Typically the *Ottawa* returned with timber from Canada, Burma or Southern USA, but she usually unloaded elsewhere in Britain (Plymouth, Liverpool etc) then went across in ballast to pick up the coal. She unloaded timber at Cardiff three times, in 1869, 1874 and 1890.

This underlines the main weakness of Cardiff as a port, and the reason for its ultimate failure, although it was a major exporter of coal by 1874, and by

1881 more was exported from there than from Newcastle.

Work had started on the West Dock in 1834, which opened five years later. This was soon outgrown by the increased size of sailing ships, and East Bute Dock was completed in 1855, followed by three more over the next 50 years. Although there was now more dock area, the lack of accommodation on the quayside still meant that the loading process was slow. Almost half of the ships were kept waiting outside the docks, and even when inside the dock system it could take sixteen hours to reach the berth. At the same time pressure on the railways meant cargos could be late arriving, which further blocked up the process, so that loading could last three weeks compared to three days at Liverpool or London. And it did in fact take the *Ottawa* three weeks in 1867, from July 30th – August 22nd, to load there.

The works were solely funded by Lord Bute for the benefit of his coal trade, and so a further problem was that there was no accommodation for unloading timber or other imports there. No merchants had wharfs on the dockside, which was restricted to the coal trade, and there were no timber ponds. Cargos must be stored in the open on the dockside, soaked in rain, mud and coal dust. The cost of moving timber either by water or truck to a distant yard added 10s a standard to costs. A ship might be 3-4 weeks unloading, compared to 6 days at Gloucester or Bristol - the *Ottawa* rarely brought imports there. This dependence on the coal industry meant that when this declined, the docks declined also.

Cardiff had another string to her bow also, as she was a major ship-repairing centre, probably the most important in country. Ships arriving in Cardiff in ballast could conveniently enter dry dock for repairs before loading a cargo, which should be ready when repairs were completed. And as we have seen in 1870 the *Ottawa* received her Lloyds Special Survey there, and was repaired, and Welsh felt and yellow metalled.

So survey and repairs completed, the *Ottawa* took on crew on 21st March, and when one James Greer failed to turn up, the Master impulsively went ashore to find him and bring him on board as they were waiting to sail. As soon as the Master returned with Greer in tow, having perhaps fished him out of the tavern, the *Ottawa* sailed for the Cape Verde Islands again, carrying 1,380 tons of coal and sundries on behalf of S. Miller and Co. Again William and George Barrett were on the crew, and Frank Pinhey was promoted to OS, at £1 per month, while wages for ABs were down again, to £2 12s 6d. Two days out in the Penarth Roads, Captain Pinhey as usual tested the skills of his men and found George Jaines quite useless and not fit to be an AB. When asked to steer, he said that he 'never had steared always cook', so he was demoted to OS at £2 a month.

The vessel arrived at St Vincent on 12th April, and, showing that life wasn't all work, on 15th the crew were allowed ashore to bathe. Now Francis Osborne, a 29 year-old Liverpudlian, started to cause trouble, claiming to be ill but actually sneaking off to drink. When the Master took him to the hospital the doctor pronounced him fit. He applied for shore leave again but it was refused on the grounds of his previous misconduct, at which he refused to work and another had to be employed in his place. After three days of this the Master took him to the Consul, who persuaded him to turn to again. Five days later, he was discharged by mutual consent, although he was in debt to the ship. No doubt he was another whom the Master was glad to see the back of. In his place another passenger was taken on, Antonio Henriques, a 22 year-old Portuguese man who wanted to go to Quebec, again at the nominal sum of 1s per month, no wages due at the end.

After a month in St Vincent the *Ottawa* went on to Quebec, probably in ballast, and on the way there was another accident, when Robert Stephens going to get a drink of water fell in the hold, and had to stay off work for a month to recover. The vessel arrived 8th June, and six men deserted as a group, clearly the work of crimps. Another was left in hospital, and one August José, following Osborne's example, went absent overnight and was brought back by a police vessel the next day, saying he needed an order for the hospital. Having been given the order, the police took him back to the hospital, who declared that there was nothing wrong with him, but he managed to slip away, and was not seen again. So although numbers were down by eight, only one crewmember was taken on at £10, no doubt because of the expense, which meant total crew numbers of 20, quite low for sailing a fully-rigged three masted ship. Taking 20 days to load this time, she came back with timber again for Restronguet, a tidal creek which is a tributary of the Carrick Roads, the estuary of the River Fal in Cornwall. During the 18th and 19th centuries Restronguet Creek was an important industrial waterway which large ships could navigate, and probably the *City of Ottawa* was bringing pit props for the tin mines of mid Cornwall. It took them three days to be towed up the river from Falmouth to Restronguet.

Pinhey paid a brief visit to Plymouth, no doubt to visit his daughter and also to sign on men for the next voyage, and on August 8th they were sent up river in a steamboat to join the ship. William Barrett was still Boatswain (although George had left by now), and Frank Pinhey's wages were raised a further 5s, while wages were generally higher, at £3 for ABs. The vessel sailed for Quebec on 11th August, arriving 8th September, and three days later while the ship was loading there, Antonio Jouy injured himself by falling from the ship onto a raft of timber, dislocating his ankle. He was taken to hospital and was left there when the ship left. Loading timber was quite a dangerous process. Sometimes it was loaded from the quay through the special timber ports in the bows that timber ships were equipped with. On this occasion, the process described by William Lord was followed[3]. He explained how, after ballast was discharged in the ballast grounds, his vessel was towed within the booms at Diamond Harbour to start loading. In Quebec felled timber was floated down river in large rafts, which were made fast besides the ship. They then became the responsibility of the officer, who marked each piece with the ship's initials to safeguard against theft. If some of the logs broke away, they had to be chased downriver and retrieved. The timber was hauled aboard through the special ports, sorted according to size for optimum storage by 'timber slingers'. Lord reports that, "these men are marvellously agile, and can balance themselves on a piece of timber, almost regardless of how much it may roll and tumble about. They have even been found venturesome enough to paddle themselves across the river. They, however, always have their timber hooks with them, which act like balancing poles. It is pleasing to listen to the stevedores when they are moving the balks of timber into their places in the ship's hold, to the stirring strains of a chant such as 'Cheerily men.'"[4]

One James Webster deserted – after the Master had gone to the trouble of paying an 18s fine to get him out of prison – so crew numbers were down to twenty again. The vessel arrived back at Liverpool Canada Dock on October 21st, and here William Barrett left the *Ottawa*. It seems he now transferred to the Royal Navy. The 1871 Census has him as Acting Chief Bosun's Mate on board the Royal Navy ship, the *Pigeon* (and still single). Over the next 10 years he married Celia, 13 years his junior, who was born at Pembroke Dock (we imagine he met her at the Naval Centre there). It is possible that he inherited money from John's will which enabled him to contemplate marrying and starting a family, as they had their first child, Ann, in 1880, and William settled ashore at 80 East Street, Plymouth, close to where he had grown up, and near to where his brother Charles lived. He was living on his naval pension, and working as a bailiff. They went on to have 6 more children, Thomas, Celia, William, Winifred, James, and Alfred, and moved to 13 St Mary Street in the same area. By 1901, William was still working as a servant, aged 61, while Thomas had left home (or died), son William was a 13-year-old errand boy, Ann was a packer at Millbay laundry, and daughter Celia a domestic servant. There was always another family unit living in the building. Clearly they were not wealthy, but William's life followed the pattern of the seafarer who settles down and has children later in life (as we have seen in the case of Samuel James Hatfield and Frederick William Withycombe).

By 5th December the *Ottawa* was loading a cargo for P Sutherland at Brunswick Dock, Liverpool. There were only three vessels loading for Aden at the same time, and by studying the dates that goods were entered for exporting there, we can conclude that the *Ottawa* was loading either bales of cotton and cotton yarn, 5 tons 2 cwt of composite metal tubes, or perhaps coal. She was cleared through Customs the next day and sailed on December 7th. No Barretts sailed this time, but Frank Pinhey's elder brother Frederick Thomas, then 24, sailed as an AB. Frederick was 12 years younger than Henry, and went to sea at the age of 17 as 'boy' so had now been sailing for seven years, previously on the Restarick ship *Eliza*.

While the *Ottawa* was still in the Liverpool river William Hood fell off the topgallant forecastle and hurt his neck. Captain Pinhey tried to persuade him to land in a steamboat or pilot boat, but he declined, saying he would soon recover, although in fact he was off duty sick until 4th January 1871, and had trouble with his neck the whole voyage. Clearly William Hood at least was on board because he wanted to be and had not been unwillingly press-ganged, or anything of that sort. But the *Ottawa* was at the start of a longer voyage.

---

1   Lloyds Agency: remarks, collisions, shipwrecks, 1860 – 1890, Banq
2   Lloyds Register 1870
3   'Reminiscences of a sailor', William R Lord, Historical Collection of the British Library, 1894
4   ibid, p23

Chapter 4

LIFE OF A SHIP: DRUNKENNESS, THEFT AND SMOKING

1871

First stop was Aden, at the Arabian Sea end of the Suez Canal. Although the Canal was opened in November 1869 (coming fully into use in 1873), it could not be used by sailing ships, but nevertheless there was an enormous appetite for coal to restock the steam ships that sailed through it, and that was probably what the *Ottawa* was carrying.

Again, if we plot the *Ottawa*'s passage by the bearings recorded in the Log Book, we find that she sailed down the coast of Africa, but apparently swung out quite wide into the mid Atlantic before rounding the Cape of Good Hope, reaching Aden on May 6th. After 20 days in port she went on for Moulmein in Burma. It took a further month to get there, and, once in Burma, she only paused for 7 days to load up with 1050 tons of teak. Teak logs were massive bulky tree-trunks, and loading would require use of the ship's heaviest tackles, and perhaps two or three elephants on the wharf[1].

Several crew members came down with dysentery, as they did on each visit there, and it seems the *Ottawa* stayed as short a time as possible. Poor William Hood was still having trouble with his neck, which now had 'rheumatism' in it, and he visited the doctor there but returned to the ship. Leaving Moulmein on July 27th or 28th, she got back to Plymouth on 27th December and remained until 31st, so Captain Pinhey could spend the Christmas period with his daughter (as the vessel did not unload there). In the meantime, the owner, Thomas Brown Restarick, was clearly having financial problems, as in April the vessel was mortgaged to William Chapell Hodge and John Ross[2], both Devonport bankers (the *City of Ottawa* was Restarick Junior's only remaining vessel by now[3]).

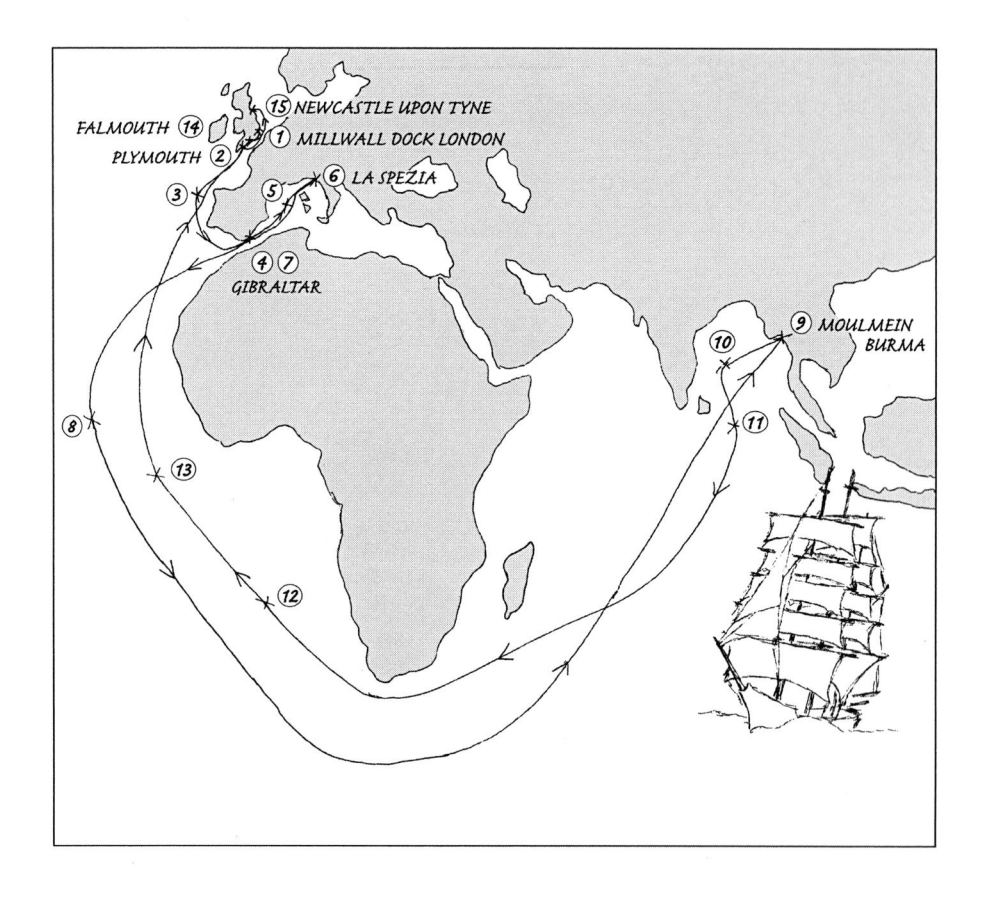

[Map showing voyage route with numbered waypoints: Newcastle Upon Tyne (15), Falmouth (14), Millwall Dock London (1), Plymouth (2), La Spezia (6), Gibraltar (4,7), Moulmein Burma (9), and other numbered points (3, 5, 8, 10, 11, 12, 13).]

1872

The *Ottawa* sailed on the last day of 1871 for London, arriving at Gravesend on 2nd January, and entering Millwall Dock the next day, where she unloaded the teak for J Rogers and Co, presumably the same J Rogers who was shortly to buy the vessel. Teak was an hard and expensive wood, then as now, used for decking on the best ships among other things. The *Ottawa* then took on ballast (she was loading at the same time as the *Cutty Sark*, incidentally), cleared customs on 18th and was towed to Gravesend by a tug on 20th, leaving at 9.00 a.m. and being moored to a buoy by 4 p.m (for a map of this voyage see Figure 5). Now Frederick Pinhey took over as Bosun and Second Mate. There

Life of a Ship: Drunkenness, Theft and Smoking

Figure 5 (facing page): Map of the voyage of the *City of Ottawa* in 1872/3, to Italy and Burma

1. Millwall Dock, London, departed 20th January 1872 in ballast
2. Plymouth, arrived 1st February, departed 8th February
3. 17 February
4. Gibraltar, 25th February
5. Charles Keates fell from the fore rigging 11th March
6. La Spezia, Italy, arrived 19th March, departed 9th May (drunkenness, prison, illness, theft …)
7. Gibraltar, 30th May
8. 16th June
9. Moulmein, Burma, arrived 18th September, departed 5th November with teak
10. 23rd November
11. 28th November, lime juice served, 'fruit once a week, currants in rice Saturday…'
12. 24th January 1873
13. 14th February
14. Falmouth, arrived 6th April
15. Newcastle upon Tyne, arrived 5th May (after being held up a month in the Channel)

was a smallpox epidemic in London at that time, and while at Gravesend two men were discharged sick, and two deserted, while a further five were taken on. They sailed two days later for Plymouth, but by 23rd the weather was looking ugly, with gale warnings issued to the South and West coasts. The *Ottawa* was now off the North Foreland and by 27th had only reached Deal in the teeth of a severe south-westerly gale, with rain and rough seas. Luckily the wind now changed and with a light following south-easterly the vessel reached Eastbourne on 28th and Plymouth by 1st February. She sailed on 8th, leaving a further three behind sick. One had 'a bad cold and fever', one was complaining of blindness (a sign of syphilis) but the symptoms of the rest were not described, although Captain Pinhey was no doubt right to be cautious, and certainly, smallpox does not seem to have taken hold on the vessel. The vessel headed first for La Spezia in Italy, having probably loaded a cargo at Plymouth, and yet another man was injured by falling from the fore rigging, Charles Keates a 31 year-old Londoner, who dislocated his wrist. The Master set it, but possibly trapped a nerve as by the time he arrived at La Spezia the muscles of his thumb were damaged and although Pinhey took him to the doctor every day for a time, he had to be left behind sick in the end. Falling from the rigging was a very frequent accident at a time when no-one wore a safety harness.

The vessel arrived at Spezia on 19th March but the crew seem to have run the Master ragged, with incidents of drunkenness, theft and general disorder. For some reason John Willcocks the steward was particularly troublesome on this occasion. Willcocks (also sometimes written Wilcocks or Wilcox) was the steward and one of the eldest crew members who sailed on more voyages on the *Ottawa* than anyone else: at least 18 voyages between 1864 and 1882 (with a couple of years missed out inbetween) and he served under four Masters: Barrett, Pinhey, Dunn and Griffin. He was illiterate and also pretty much innumerate, as his recorded ages in the crew lists vary wildly between 41 and 57, but not in chronological order! In fact from the baptismal records it seems he was born on 19 April 1819 in Fowey, Cornwall, and from his seaman's ticket that he went to sea at the age of 22 in 1841, as 'boy'. He was quite short at 5ft 3½in, with black hair, dark complexion and brown eyes, and had JW (his initials) tattooed on his right arm. He spent 2½ years in the Foreign Service (on long-haul merchant vessels) and gave his address as 'Liverpool when unemployed' in 1847. Around this time he married Jane Wickett, daughter of a naval seaman of Prussian origin, and in 1851 is recorded as living at 1 Woolster Street, Plymouth with the lady and her parents, also John and Jane. By 1861 they had a son, Samuel, born 1858, and were living at 10 Lower Batter Street, Plymouth with grandmother Jane, now widowed, and her nine-year-old nephew William J Morcomb. When John Willcocks entered the *Ottawa* records in January 1864, he was aged 45, and had previously sailed on the *Princess Royal*, part of the Restarick fleet. In 1868 he had spent a month in hospital in Moulmein, Burma, for an unspecified illness, then he missed the next two voyages, sailing on the *Eliza*, also a Restarick vessel before rejoining the *Ottawa*.

Ten days after arriving in La Spezia, Pinhey recorded that John Willcocks 'was continually neglecting his duty and going to bed.' By April 9th, Pinhey was 'obliged to take John Willcocks to a place of safety, not being capable of taking care of himself through drink. The British Consul put him in the jail'. But he was out by 11th, promising not to drink any more. Sadly this was untrue, and on 13th he was back in prison for 'again neglecting his duty and getting intoxicated, laying on the shore in an insensible state'. Pinhey, showing great forbearance, took him out again two days later, as he again promised to be good, but the temptations of Italian wine were too great and he was drunk again by 18th. The Log Books do not record that Willcocks misbehaved again on subsequent voyages, and his wage rates increase steadily throughout his working life, starting at £3 7d 6d a month in 1864, and rising steadily to a peak of £5 10s a month in 1879, even though the wages levels of ABs did not. He was receiving a loyalty bonus, and this implies that his behaviour was overall not too outrageous, so perhaps this episode in La Spezia was the exception rather than the rule. He generally managed to bring home a moderate sum as the balance of his wages to take home to his family and was usually amongst the most provident on board.

La Spezia had a large naval base and John Ridley managed to annoy the naval officers as much as he irritated Pinhey, as he ended up in jail for 'insolence to officer on guard and smoking which is prohibited' – fire was of course a hazard with wooden ships and potentially inflammable cargos. Then Pinhey discovered while fitting out the ship at the end of April that a large quantity of running gear blocks and other items had been taken from the ship (these were the pulleys that enabled the sails to be raised and lowered etc). This may have been a spot of private enterprise by crew members, or may have been by outsiders: William Lord records a remarkably similar incident which occurred in 1879 in China, when, finding the nightwatchman asleep, river thieves crept aboard and cast off all the braces and other running gear belayed on the topgallants rail, then dropped the end quietly overboard; these sailed away on tide and the thieves cut them off as close to the ship as they dared, and got away with the booty.

The ship sailed on 3rd May. It is interesting that no-one had deserted here, so clearly La Spezia was not seen as a good place to remain in, but conversely all the troublemakers and discontented remained on board, causing problems. Two replacements were taken on at Genoa, at the same rate as those who joined at London, £2 10s. As the Suez Canal was not open to her, the *City of Ottawa* sailed back through the Mediterranean and round Africa again for Burma. As can be seen from the map, after passing through the doldrums, the area of calm, windless water around the Equator, the vessel swung quite widely to the West towards to coast of Brazil, pushed by the southeast trade winds, which was quite a common occurrence when sailing southwards through the Atlantic. Then she swung widely round the coast of South Africa to pick up the westerly currents prevalent in the southern hemisphere, before heading up through the Indian Ocean to Moulmein (where she again picked up a cargo of teak, arriving 18th September and leaving 5th November. Two men were taken on here at the slightly higher rate of £3 and £3 5s. Once more there was sickness: crew suffered from fever, ague and dysentery, and it seemed to be especially the ones who had got in trouble in La Spezia: Willcocks spent three days in hospital with fever. Neil Walford managed to get in trouble even in Burma and was brought on board by the police, to whom Pinhey had to pay five rupees. Perhaps because of the incidents of sickness, it was on this occasion that Pinhey noted in the Log that on 27th November (while still in the Bay of Bengal) he served lime juice and next day 'from leaving port served preserved meats and potatoes or yams, fruit once a week, currants in rice Saturday'. Heading back to Britain, the *Ottawa* clung more closely to the coast of Africa.

1873

Although bound for Newcastle, the vessel stopped off at Falmouth on 6th April, after having been at sea for nearly 15 months. The same group who had caused problems in La Spezia were still being uncooperative, claiming to be unable to work through illness, though Captain Pinhey was sceptical. After 7 days in Falmouth – perhaps to allow the Captain to see his daughter again - the ship sailed for Newcastle, but was held up in the channel windbound, together with a large fleet of ships, until the beginning of May, and only arrived in Newcastle, probably at North Shields, on 5th May towed by the steam tug *Victoria*, which had to stop at Bridlington to take on coal. After unloading the teak, the vessel was surveyed and on 22nd at the age of 27 Frederick Pinhey took advantage of the stay to take his Only Mate's Certificate, passing on all counts. He gave his address as 25 King Street, South Shields, which must have been a lodging house. We imagine he was encouraged, trained, perhaps even given financial aid, by his elder brother.

A Note on Newcastle

The *Ottawa* actually went to the Port of Newcastle three times, though each time in fact she probably only got as far as either North or South Shields at the mouth of the river. She brought in timber, once from Mobile in the southern USA and twice high grade teak from Burma for use in Newcastle industry: it could be used for ship's decks. It is not recorded that she brought a cargo away. Coal exports were mainly in the hands of the local collier ships.

Newcastle was quite a hazardous destination: large numbers of ships were lost sailing up the East Coast, largely because the shipping lanes were so crowded[4] as was shown by the fate of William Bunker, and more foundered outside Newcastle because of the lack of a safe harbour during high winds[5].

Seamen arriving in North Shields often stayed at the Northumberland Arms, a large sailor's home on the quayside. Formerly the town house of the Duke of Northumberland, it was adapted in 1854-6 to accommodate 80 visiting seamen and called 'the Jungle' because of the stuffed animal heads and trophies (Plate vii). It is nice to think of our crew admiring them, though we know that Frederick Pinhey at least stayed in South Shields while he studied for his Mate's exam.

The *Ottawa* set off for Quebec on June 2nd with Frederick as Second Mate, arriving there 1st August. In the meantime on 19th July the vessel had been sold to John Porter Rogers of Fenchurch Street, London, although she continued to be registered in Plymouth. John Porter Rogers was already a merchant, but he bought the *Nimrod* at about the same time and ran the two ships simultaneously for most of the rest of the century. The *Nimrod* was another sailing ship but smaller and older than the *Ottawa*: she was 695 tons, built at Medford, New Jersey, in the US, in 1855. By coincidence (presumably) John Barrett had been the *Nimrod*'s Master after leaving the *Ottawa*. Had he mentioned to Rogers what a good ship the *Ottawa* was?

To celebrate the change of ownership, pay was increased to a high for ABs of £4 and £4 5s. Nevertheless one man still deserted at Quebec. The *Ottawa* was there during a highly destructive hurricane[6] and Captain Pinhey had to deal with several medical emergencies: again one man fell from the ship while loading, three others had dysentery, and the Captain spent quite a lot of time taking men to the hospital and back. It was also during this eventful visit, on 27th August, that Captain Pinhey married for the second time, to Louisa Adams who was 31 (Pinhey was 39). Louisa was born in Quebec but the family considered themselves English, not French, and she was from the same social class as Henry, as her father was a coal merchant. Although we do not know when they met, Pinhey had been in Quebec twice in 1870, but then had not been back in the intervening two years, so perhaps the lovers seized the chance while he was there. Courtship could not have been easy with no long-distance telephones, Skype, etc. Captain Pinhey must have been pleased that at least one member of his family, Frederick, could be present, although he is not named as a witness at the wedding.

Unfortunately he had very little time to celebrate, as the next day we find he was working out the wages due to Nils Linderholm and Orlof Henderson, as they were too ill to travel, and sending their clothes to the hospital. He laid on three new crew members to replace the sick and the deserter, two ABs at £10 and an OS at £7. The vessel sailed the day after. Quite probably Louisa accompanied her husband, although the practise was rather frowned upon and certainly she does not appear on the documentation. If she was left behind, she may have wondered if she had imagined the wedding, as Pinhey did not return to Quebec for a year.

On the first day at sea Pinhey tested the new men, and reduced the pay of OS John Ross from £7 to £5 because he could not steer, and was 'backward in many respects'. The ship returned to Portsmouth on 20th September, and a month later left in ballast, the men being taken on by boat while the *Ottawa* was anchored at Spithead, sailing three days later on 19th October for Pensacola, America, into a light westerly breeze. By 21st October the wind was heading WSW strong, and the vessel anchored off Torbay until 25th, when they could get underway. The ship also took on an apprentice again, Harry Mansfield from London, 17 and on his first ship (there had been no apprentices over the last six years). Wages had fallen back again, to £3 17s 6d and £3 15s.

The ship had not been long at sea when tragedy struck. Ten days out and still off the coast of Portugal, John Betty, the cook, died suddenly of asthma. He had been sick on and off since leaving port, but had his own medication. At 9.00 p.m. he appeared fine and told the Captain he was 'first rate', but then at 10.00 p.m. he suddenly had an attack, and died, and we can sense that there was a sense of shock on board. The ship hove to, and next morning at 8.00 a.m. he was buried at sea, sewn in canvas, in the presence of all the crew, Captain Pinhey reading the burial service. It is sometimes said that sailors who died at sea were disposed of without ceremony, but this seems a touchingly meaningful rite, as orchestrated by the sensitive captain. John Betty was 50 years old at the time of his death, was born at Stonehouse, Plymouth, and had a dark complexion, brown hair, blue eyes, and smallpox scars. He was quite short, being 5ft 2in, and first went to sea at the age of 22 to be a cook in the Royal Navy. At 31 he married Maria, also from Stonehouse, and they lived at the same address there, on St Mary's Street, until he died. It must have been a poor area with a very high population per building, but Maria could not have been too lonely when he was at sea as several of her neighbours were wives of mariners. John Betty had only just left the Navy – perhaps he had been invalided out – and the *Ottawa* may have been his first civilian ship.

Pinhey did not move with indecent haste to auction off his possessions, leaving it to the following January. In addition to clothes and bedding, John Betty showed evidence of some sophistication, carrying a small box containing one ring and sundry small articles, an album (of photos and keepsakes?), and four books (more details can be found in Chapter 8). The sale of his property only realised £2 8s, and he had only accrued sixteen days of back pay, which came to the same amount, so when the advance on his wages was deducted, plus a shipping fee of 1s, that left only 5s to be handed on to his wife. This does not seem much for a professional life spent at sea, but hopefully she also got his ring and books.

The ship continued down the coast of Africa, before crossing the Atlantic, arriving in Pensacola in the Southern USA on December 8th, where seven men deserted, though not all at the same time. Pensacola was a popular port for men to leave, as there was already a large transient population of seamen, and the possibility of higher wages, but perhaps also having had a death at sea the men felt the *Ottawa* was unlucky?

1874 – FROM 'SHIP' TO 'BARQUE'

Eight more men were taken on in Pensacola at £9 a month for ABs, and ended up with a good sum at the end, after six weeks at sea. The *Ottawa* left on 8th January after just a month in port over Christmas and the New Year. Two weeks before the *Ottawa* arrived at Plymouth, yet again there was an accident when, with 'a heavy sea running and the wind flying all around the compass' and with two men at the wheel, James McKae was thrown over the wheel and broke his right leg and left knee cap[7]. Presumably it was in this bad weather that the vessel lost her mizzen topgallant mast, as she was so described when she was noted passing the Lizard at the southern tip of Cornwall on February 20th heading eastwards.

She arrived at Plymouth on 21st February and it was almost certainly[8] now that her rigging was changed from 'full-rigged three masted ship' to 'barque'. In other words, the third mast, the mizzen, was changed to a 'fore-and-aft' rigging, which made the vessel easier to manage and required less men to sail her. Many of the old full rigged merchant vessels were being modified in this way. The vessel was surveyed in March, and at this point the Lloyds Register recorded that her A1 rating was 'expired', although it was to be several years before she had her special survey to determine her new rating.

The repairs and survey must have been carried out very quickly as she sailed on March 3rd, after a stay of only ten days, in ballast. The Mate William Bunker had left the vessel at Plymouth - perhaps he felt it was time for his own command, but he came to a sad end – see Chapter 7 for details.

Second Mate Frederick Pinhey did not rejoin the *Ottawa* either. He went on to be Mate on the *Camelford*, sailing to Hamburg, then Second Mate on the *Bayswater* and *Albuna*, sailing to Java and India, and then as Mate on the *Jumina*, which was a tramp ship, away from home ports for four years. We know that in 1878 the vessel was involved in a bad storm sailing from China to Australia, when she shipped a heavy sea which flooded the front of the cabin, damaging the berths and all that was stored there, as Frederick had to apply for another copy of his Mate's Certificate. He never went on to take the Captain's Certificate and died on 26th September 1883, aged only 37, although his age was estimated to be 42 on the death certificate, which implies he looked rather older. He was living in a Lodging House in Whitehouse in the London Docklands area, and died suddenly, of 'rupture of a blood vessel of the lungs', so perhaps he had a bad cough and was a heavy smoker. There does not seem to have been any family around or close friends since no-one knew his age. Perhaps if he had lived longer he might have taken the Master's examination like his older brother. On the other hand Frank Pinhey returned to the *City of Ottawa* still as an AB after missing the last two voyages when he had been sailing on the *Ethel* of Hull instead.

The *Ottawa* arrived at Doboy, in the Southern USA, on 10th April to take on a load of timber for Greenock. Her draft was recorded as 13ft aft, 12ft forward when in ballast, and 18ft 10in aft, 18ft forward, when loaded[9]. This time the journey was relatively uneventful, with no desertions or accidents, and only John Dawson was sick, suffering chronically from fever and ague. The *Ottawa* arrived at Greenock on June 13th, which means that this was a very quick passage there and back of only just over three months.

On July 8th at 6 in the evening the *Ottawa* was towed from the dock to off Greenock, but was delayed as two crew members had not joined. The next day one of these still had not shown, so Robert Buchanan, an 18 year old Glasgow lad, was taken on in some haste and the ship sailed for Quebec with 799 tons of coal to the value of £450[10]. It turned out that Robert Buchanan was not an OS as he claimed, but rather a boy running away to sea, because when the Captain tested his competence he was downgraded to 'boy' at £2 a month. Then another lad was found, a stowaway who had sneaked on board at Greenock, with the very Scottish name of Charles Henry Logan. Total crew numbers had been steadily dropping after she had become a barque, and they

Life of a Ship: Drunkenness, Theft and Smoking

now numbered 18 plus two apprentices.

The vessel was held back by the wind and only arrived at Quebec on 25th August, where the stowaway Charles Henry Logan left the ship. Captain Pinhey (and perhaps his wife) had been away for a year and he managed to stay there for a month. But although no-one deserted this visit, instead Pinhey had a lot of trouble with violence and abusive incidents. Generally it seems that when trouble arose on board, it would be centred on two or three troublemakers, and this time he had two pairs of them. John Woods was the cook mentioned above who took exception to being kept waiting by the officers lingering over lunch. Six days later the Mate heard shouting and went to investigate, on which the cook, joined by Charles Adams, started to abuse him too, and they were making so much noise that the police came aboard and took them off to prison. The Mate was David Sloane, a 49 year-old Scotsman, who was possibly not popular, and the cook was 42, so ought to have known better. Pinhey brought them out the next day, thinking they would have learnt their lesson (and because he had to pay for labourers to unload and load in their place), and they promised to behave themselves. But when he tried the same ploy with John Dwyer it didn't work. Dwyer was 36, an Irishman from Waterford, who repeatedly went ashore without leave and came back drunk and abusive. Pinhey had him committed to jail for four weeks, but brought him out after eleven days at a cost of £6 5s 0d, 'thinking he would be better'. But on 25th September he was off again at 7.30 in the morning, together with a younger Waterford man called James O'Brian, and Pinhey had Dwyer committed to jail again. Pinhey returning on board at 11.00 a.m. found that O'Brian had drunkenly raised the flag for the police, and he slung him in the cabin where he fell asleep. But the same day he took him to jail as well and had the two of them confined there until the ship sailed next day. The Police were generally happy to release prisoners back to their ship rather than having the expense of continuing to look after them themselves. It is almost impressive that the seamen could get so drunk so early in the morning.

The *Ottawa* sailed for Cardiff on 26th September, arriving on 23rd October at the East Bute Dock, where she took two months to unload and to take on a cargo of 1140 tons of coal for Worms and Co. Cardiff East Bute Dock was notoriously slow. However now Pinhey left, to take his daughter to Canada to live with his new wife, and turned his back on long distance voyages, for a while at least – for the rest of his story, see Chapter 7. Pinhey had not generally been as speedy a navigator, nor as ruthless as John Barrett, and seems to have been a conscientious and compassionate man, very fond of his family, and he definitely had more problems with bad behaviour and drunkenness. This is also the end of the surviving series of logbooks, although some later crew lists remain, so we can no longer listen in to the fascinating saga of misdemeanours, bad behaviour, illness and accident that characterised the Pinhey years.

---

1. 'Joseph Conrad, Master Mariner', Peter Villiers, Seafarer Books, 2006
2. Lloyds Register of Registrations, 1863, Plymouth and West Devon Record Office
3. 'Plymouth's other fleet – The Merchant Shipping Registers of the Port of Plymouth', unpublished CD by Gareth E. Hicks
4. 'East Coast Shipping', A A C Hedges, Shire Publications Ltd 1974
5. 'The Shipping Industry: life and death at sea', G Patterson, in 'The Great Age Of Industry In The North East' ed R W Sturgess, Durham County Local History Society, 1981
6. 'Masters Under God. Makers of Empire 1816 – 1884' in 'A History of the British Merchant Navy Volume 3', Richard Woodman, The History Press 2009
7. Log Book, 1874, Devon Record Office, Exeter
8. This was almost certainly the time that the ship was modified. Before this sightings generally identified her as 'ship', afterwards as 'barque'.
9. Log book, 1874, Devon Record Office, Exeter
10. Customs, Bills of Entry, Clyde, 1874, Merseyside Maritime Museum

Chapter 5

LIFE OF A SHIP: MIDDLE YEARS

1874 CONTINUED

William Dunn took over as Master, the third to come from Devon. He was born at Wembury in 1844, and in 1851 was living with his widowed mother Maria, who was a pauper, and his three sisters Eliza, Ann and Emma, who seem to have died young. Perhaps this explains why he went to sea as a 'boy' in 1855, aged only 11 – he wasn't indentured, like Barrett and Pinhey. Nevertheless, he spent 6 years as Ordinary Seaman learning his trade, then 4 years as AB before taking his examination as Second Mate aged 20, First Mate three years later, and received his Captain's Certificate of Competency aged 26. He continued to sail as Mate to Canada and the USA before taking over the *Ottawa* in 1874, aged 30, his first ship as Master.

The ship sailed on 25th December – Christmas does not seem to have been a festival much regarded in the merchant shipping business.

A Note on Crew Numbers

The number of crew laid on each voyage started off, when the *Ottawa* was young and profitable, at around 26, plus three apprentices. The vessel sometimes returned somewhat shorthanded from Quebec because of the high wage rates demanded there, for instance in 1869, numbers were down to 18, as ten deserted there and only five were taken on.

Roster numbers fell generally, to around 22 men per voyage until 1874, when the vessel became a barque. As this configuration required less men, in that year numbers fell to 18 plus two apprentices. In 1880 the short passage home to Plymouth from Le Havre involved ten men, and by 1888, when the owner was struggling financially, we have the impression that he was attempting to screw every last penny from the vessel, and she twice sailed back from Quebec with only ten or eleven men, and they were paid only the lowest wages. By now the best crews were going to steamers, and perhaps also the Master had to make do with the seamen available.

1875

The *Ottawa* arrived at Rio di Janiero on March 4th to unload the coal (after a journey of only two months) then left on April 12th to go northwards up the coast of South America to Pensacola for timber, setting off home on 9th July and arriving in King Road at Bristol on 25th August. There she was probably towed up the River Severn (which was difficult to navigate for large sailing ships) to Sharpness Point where she arrived on 30th. Until 25th November 1874, only nine months previously, vessels had to navigate the difficult entry into the old dock, but by now the new docks, which could take much larger ships, had just opened so the *Ottawa* was right at the cutting edge of modern technology on this occasion[1]! She would probably have part of her load removed at Sharpness to reduce her draught (see Figure 6), then be towed up the canal to Gloucester Docks by a steam tug to unload at the timber yards there – horse drawn tugs had been replaced in the 1860s. It must have been an amazing experience, to see large vessels apparently floating through the middle of the countryside, for the canal is set in lovely scenery. The vessel was in port in Gloucester for over a month (see Plate ix) and departed on 30th September, almost certainly in ballast, because it was very difficult to pick up a cargo there. George Griffin, later to be Master, joined now as Second Mate and Frank Pinhey sailed for one last time on the *Ottawa* – he had left with his brother Henry in 1874 to join the *Bell* at Liverpool, but after this he disappears from the records. Wages were up to £3 15s: they were generally higher under Dunn. The vessel headed for Pensacola, arriving 21st December.

1876

She probably picked up timber at Pensacola and was cleared through customs on 22nd January, but had a rough journey back and put into Liverpool on March 3rd without her wheelhouse and a portion of the bulwarks, having shipped a heavy sea during a gale. This shows the dangers that wooden ships were subject to, but also the skill of the crew on board who could clearly patch her up sufficiently to get back to port.

Figure 6: Boats at Sharpness, showing rafts of timber in the foreground.
Reproduced courtesy of Gloucestershire Archives, ref. SR9/49274

A Note on Liverpool

In some ports, very little remains of the original merchant dock system – Newport, or Cardiff for instance – just as very few merchant sailing ships, as opposed to naval vessels, are now remembered.

Liverpool, though, is exceptional in still keeping most of its old dock system, and using and improving it. The Old Dock, the first enclosed dock in the country, built in 1707, has been preserved under a new shopping centre, and is now quite a distance from the water's edge, showing how the river has altered over the years. The dock system evolved slowly, but at its greatest measured an amazing seven miles long in a narrow strip along the edge of the Mersey, second in size only to London. With a tidal range of 30ft, which left a narrow window for ships to enter, the port from 1811 evolved the system of 'half-tide' basins with an outer lock gate and lower sill so that vessels had more time to manoeuvre. Vessels would anchor in the river, then negotiate to be towed in by steam tug, but were probably winched in for the last part of the process. The story of the collision with the *Carrier Dove* mentioned above gives more insight into the system.

The *City of Ottawa* visited Liverpool some twelve times, mostly with timber.

On her first visit she unloaded at Sandon Dock, where she would follow the Liverpool practise of unloading timber directly onto the quay (as opposed to unloading into timber ponds as in London). From 1835 the Liverpool and Manchester Railway Company was building a line along the eastern quays specifically for the timber trade. The next couple of times the *Ottawa* unloaded a mixed cargo from India (including the bison horns and head!) at the Albert Dock, now the site of Tate Liverpool, (see Plate x) but after that she always brought timber from Canada or the southern USA, and usually docked at the Canada Dock, which was built specifically for that purpose (it still deals with timber today). She often sailed outwards in ballast, but three times had an unidentified cargo.

There was also a good system of graving docks where ships could be surveyed, fitted out and if necessary repaired, as happened to the *Ottawa* five times, including probably the present visit of 1876 when she had sustained damage at sea.

Liverpool continued to build docks throughout the century, and from the 1880s improvements were made which included pumping in water to raise or maintain water levels and reducing the number of dock entrances but increasing internal communication channels between them, as silting was always a problem. The Dock Commissioners never quite managed to keep up with developments and make them profitable, their problems compounded by restrictive union practices, and by the end of the century were left with far more dock space than the trade actually required.

Many of the docks have now been refurbished and some of the warehouses have been converted into very classy flats, but many are unused and still maintain their original appearance, of interest to the student of Victorian archaeology.

Having been probably patched up very quickly in Liverpool, the *Ottawa* continued on her way to Barrow, arriving 13th March, and on 12th April left for a very quick return journey to Quebec for timber, which she was unloading at Greenock by July 12th. There were no deserters during this visit to Quebec, but wages were good: £4 5s a month. At Greenock she loaded in two weeks and headed back to Quebec with 413 tons of coal valued at £185, which implies that the cost of coal had risen from £1 15s a ton in 1874 to £2 5s a ton two years later. Again there were high wages and no deserters, and six days out at sea the remaining apprentice, Joseph George Jury, having reached the end of the term of his indenture, was made Third Mate at £4 6s a month. For more on Jury's life, see Chapter 8. The *Ottawa* arrived in Quebec on September 3rd and a sailor from Prince Edward Island was discharged by mutual agreement. Unfortunately his replacement John Kelso was committed to gaol for ten weeks for refusing to sail, which sounds like he could be an example of the practice of crimps bundling a man on board drunk, although on this occasion he sobered up in time to insist on quitting the ship before she sailed. The vessel cleared on 21st September and arrived at Barrow a month later, times which rivalled those achieved by Barrett in her prime.

1877–8

By coincidence it was this year, on January 5th 1877, that Barrett died on the *Ribble* at Queenstown, Ireland.

The *Ottawa* remained in Barrow until April, having some repairs and the again overdue Special Survey to assess her classification. The Lloyds Registers[2] where this is recorded are not easy to interpret, but it seems that the vessel had been avoiding this for some three years, probably because she was beginning to deteriorate. She had been recorded as 'unclassified' since 1874 and now instead of A1 she now received a rating of AE1. The AE rating indicated a ship 'found on survey fit for the safe conveyance of dry and perishable good on shorter voyages, and for the conveyance of cargoes not in their nature subject to sea damage on any voyage'. In fact, the *Ottawa* had been conveying bulk cargos of coal and timber for some time, and so was probably not too affected in terms of her business, although it was now that she stopped carrying apprentices again. At this point also George Griffin was made up to First Mate, and the former apprentice Joseph George Jury became Second Mate. Dunn seems to have been very encouraging to protégées.

George Griffin had been born in 1850 in West Buckland, Somerset, to a non-nautical, unprivileged family: his father John was an agricultural labourer, and mother Mary Ann was illiterate. Possibly his family moved around wherever the work was to be found, as they do not appear in the Census records. George went to sea as 'boy' at 15. After his first passage he sailed for 7 years as Ordinary Seaman, then became AB at 22. The last ship he sailed on before the *Ottawa* was the *Sobraon*, which was a very good, high class ship involved in the passenger trade to Australia, one that people might join as a convalescence cruise[3]. He was evidently well thought of and encouraged, as he then took his Second Mate's Certificate and joined the *Ottawa* in 1875. Two years later, while the ship was being repaired in Barrow, he went to Plymouth and took his First Mate's Certificate on 11th January. By April he had rejoined the vessel, and was made up to First Mate. Considering he had not started his career by being indentured, this shows how quickly a suitable and hard working young man could rise through the ranks.

In 1877 the *Ottawa* again had two fast passages to Canada. She sailed on 17th April in ballast, arriving 18th May, sailed 8th June, back to Barrow on 7th July, sailed again on 27th, this time going no further than North Sydney in Nova Scotia, and back to Liverpool Canada Dock with timber by 27th October. On December 18th she sailed for St Thomas in the West Indies (now the Virgin Islands) arriving 24th January 1878. There is no record that she took on any cargo in Liverpool, a port for which a good set of Customs House Documents exists, so it seems likely that she had an order to take a load from St Thomas to Doboy, USA, as she made a very similar journey on her next voyage. She stayed in St Thomas for two weeks before heading for the mainland, arriving February 11th at Darien (close to Doboy) and leaving on March 12th. Here she picked up a good cargo of timber, comprising 367 logs of spruce timber, or a total of 4123 ft, which makes each log approximately 10ft long. She arrived with this in Liverpool on 29th April and anchored in the river while waiting for a berth, probably in Canada Dock. The logs were imported by Farnworth and Jardine Wood, Brokers of Liverpool, who for some reason did not advertise them for sale in the Liverpool Mercury until October 15th.[4] The *Ottawa* was surveyed in Liverpool in June, then went on to Cardiff in ballast for 1260 tons of coal, for H Worms. After eight days loading she sailed on 20th June for Rio di Janeiro, arriving 24th August, then going from there to St Thomas again, where presumably she picked up a cargo for Pensacola, arriving there on 9th December. There may have been an epidemic in Rio, as two crew were left behind sick, and one crew member who joined there was sick by the time the vessel arrived in Pensacola. Five deserted at Rio, although the replacements taken on received only 10s more. However the further two who deserted at Pensacola perhaps fared better, as their replacements received a whole £1 more than the original crewmembers, or £4 per month. But generally the wage differentials between ports were being reduced at that time.

1879

She was cleared for Liverpool on 11th January, arriving in the river at Liverpool on 3rd March and clearing customs the next day, this time carrying 461 pallets of hewn and 168 pallets of sawn pitch pine, and 531 pallets of deals for P Sutherland Junior and Co. She was surveyed again in June. At this point Dunn left the *Ottawa*. He had sailed his ship quickly, but also paid reasonable wages above the lowest rates, and clearly was encouraging to the young men in his care and was repaid by several of his officers and crew remaining from one ship to the next. He next sailed on the *Eleanor* then the *James Duncan*, and it was on this ship that he sailed to South America but died at sea at Santos, Brazil[5], on 2nd January 1882, aged 38, of apoplexy, only three years after leaving the *Ottawa*. This was a young age to die of a heart attack or stroke, and perhaps shows how stressful the job of Master could be with long hours, constant pressure of work etc[6]. At any rate he left a personal estate of £272 18s (worth today £21,400, or £175,000 in terms of economic status), quite a good sum. It seems Dunn never married and had no living relatives, as his executor was Thomas Showan, a retired schoolmaster living in Widnes, Lancashire. He must have been an old school friend, as they were not linked by marriage, but both grew up in the Plymouth area in very poor circumstances (Thomas' mother remarried and he was brought up in the home of his stepfather, a labourer in the dockyard, in a street where many were paupers. His sister was less fortunate, as she was brought up in the Plymouth workhouse). Dunn did well to rise from such an impoverished early life to the position of Master, and it is interesting that a good education was available for bright but poor youths in that area, as also shown in the parallel career of his friend. Possibly poor nutrition in early youth was a factor in Dunn's early death.

Frederick Lyle was due to take over after Dunn, but he only spent one day on board before he left, sick. He was already 51, and had been born in Hanover. He took his examination for Only Mate in 1854, although he failed to produce the necessary documentation to prove his years at sea, as he had lost them when shipwrecked. Clearly he wasn't very good at paperwork, as when he took his Master's Certificate in 1861, some of it was missing. In the years before he almost sailed on the *Ottawa*, he was Master of the *Nimrod* on long-haul voyages to the East Indies, although this was not the one owned by John Porter Rogers, owner of the *Ottawa*, but another ship of the same name. Lyle was married, with 3 sons and 1 daughter (1 son died before the age of 10), who grew up in Bedminster, Bristol. One of his sons, Freeman, grew up to be a Factory Time Keeper and named his son after his father. It does not seem that Frederick ever sailed again on leaving the *Ottawa* and he was found dead only a year and a half later under mysterious circumstances. He had been missing for a fortnight when his body was found face down in the mud by the River Avon, near the suspension bridge, on 19th November 1881. Henry Preston, presumably a friend, said that he 'believed he had nothing whatever on his mind, but he was somewhat given to drink'[7]. He had last been seen alive on 5th November 'on board one of the steamers going to Hotwells'[8]. Hotwells is across the river from his home in Bedminster, so the implication seems to be that he probably wasn't suicidal, but perhaps fell off the ferry into the river when drunk. A verdict of 'found drowned' was passed.

To return to June 1880, the illness of Frederick Lyle was a stroke of luck for George Griffin. Clearly well thought of by Dunn, it seems he had been encouraged to apply for his Certificate of Competence as Master, which he had just received on 13th June in Plymouth. On 26th June, the same day that Lyle left, Griffin took over and the ship was cleared through customs. But by the next day the barometer was falling, with a gale warning on the North and West coasts, strong south-westerly winds and dull unsettled weather, and it seems Griffin decided to wait a while. The sea continued to be rough until the 29th, when it was cloudy with a light westerly wind, and the *Ottawa* sailed on the 30th.

Held up by Gales

Oldfashioned sailing ships were handicapped by their inability to contend successfully with strong head winds9. After a succession of north-west gales, the River Mersey and docks would become crowded with outward bound ships waiting for a shift of wind to enable them to get away, and when this took place the river could be filled with as many as 300 sailing ships of all sorts and sizes, working their way out to sea on the ebb tide, with a number being towed. On the other hand, during easterly gales, which prevailed in November and December and in the Spring, the docks could be closed for weeks together, with few or no vessels entering. The inward bound fleet would be caught in the estuary, and had to stay there until the wind changed. We have seen above also that many ships could be trapped by adverse gales in the English Channel.

The ship sailed in ballast for Pensacola, arriving 23rd August. Wage levels were lower again, only £2 10s, and it seems wages were lower globally this year as replacements taken on in Pensacola now only received £3 10s. One of the men taken on in Pensacola, Robert Purves, was disembarked there also as he 'joined the ship on 20th in state of intoxication and from such cause has been since incapacitated and become sick. Left behind through his own default no wages due and his effects have been returned to him.' This sounds like he had been bundled on board drunk by crimps, but in this instance sickness was perhaps mistaken for drunkenness, or alternatively whatever the gentleman had been drinking had itself made him ill. It is interesting that the fact he joined drunk was not a matter for comment, just that he then did not sober up. After a stay of one month in Pensacola, the vessel cleared customs heading for Barrow, probably with timber, arriving after a short stop in Liverpool on 17th November.

1880

She went on to Cardiff, probably for coal, arriving 27th January, sailing a month later for Rio di Janeiro. On this voyage, the *Ottawa* sailed with a crew of 16 men, but this included Samuel Willcocks, son of the steward John. John's wife Jane had died on 12th February 1880 at the family home at 8 Lower Batter Street of bronchitis, heart problems and dropsy, and son Samuel is listed as 'present at the death', though quite likely John was there too, as he was in port at the time. By the 20th, Samuel Willcocks, who was now aged 22, had signed up with his father, and sailed as a cook on his first (and quite probably only) ship at £2 per month.

The *Ottawa* arrived in Rio on 21st April then sailed for Mobile, where she arrived 9th July, but was promptly put into quarantine until 20th when she was declared free of disease. She was cleared for Le Havre carrying timber on 26th August, but on October 30th limped into Plymouth, having 'lost her mainyard, mainlowertopsail yard, bulwarks, skylight, tanks, compasses, sails and deckload, and making water; the vessel was badly strained, having experienced terrific weather during the passage[10]'. The damage indicates that she was showing her age, and was more easily affected by bad weather. It must have been a terrifying experience for the crew, and the survival of the ship and those on board her must have depended on both luck and good seamanship. At the beginning of November the strong gales continued[11], and on 9th November, only 10 days later and clearly not entirely repaired, she was towed to Le Havre, arriving in two days. Even then her problems were not over, for in Le Havre she 'broke adrift in the night from her moorings and carried away the mast and bowsprit of a French smack, also staving in the boat and breaking in the main rail of a French steamer and damaging her own bows' – which must have been a very expensive experience for the owner. In Le Havre the crew was discharged and Samuel Willcocks went home with £14 4s 4d, in his pocket. He raced home to his sweetheart Beatrice and was married just over a month later on 19th December at Charles Parish Church, Plymouth, in the presence of her parents. Clearly the experience destroyed any temptation Samuel might have had to sail again, for by the time the census was returned the next April Samuel was living in his new home at 38 Albert Street with his wife, and working as a carpenter, set up with quite a nice nest egg.

It is possible that John Willcocks was not present as he was still on the *Ottawa* when she sailed back for Plymouth after unloading the rest of her cargo. She left on 31st December with ten men taken on in France, plus the Second Mate and Steward. Instead of being paid per month, they received a fee of £2 10s each for the journey payable on completion which was not a bad sum for six days' sailing, and did not restock with fresh food, as existing stock was deemed 'sufficient without waste'.

A Note on Wages

Wages were generally paid per month, although the amount earned was calculated per days worked. The highest paid crewmembers (after the Master, whose earnings or profits are not given on the crew lists) were the Mate and the Carpenter (sometimes one, sometimes the other). Next would come the Bosun, the Sailmaker, the Steward and Cook, often in that order. For instance on the 1866 voyage Newport to Bombay (Mumbai), the Mate received £6 10s a month, the carpenter £6, the Bosun £4 5s, the Sailmaker £4, the Steward £3 10s, the Cook £2 17s 6d (although he did not join, and the ship seems to have sailed without a cook at all). The Bosun's Mate received £3 per month, and the Carpenter's Mate £4. On that voyage, an AB would receive £2 15s, and an OS £2 5s. It is very difficult to give an equivalent value in today's money, as there are so many economic variables, but we might consider that in terms of average earnings then and now, an AB would be receiving approximately £1,550 per month, which equals £18,600 per annum[12] (although this was only payable when he was actually working, of course). It is interesting that over the thirty year period covered by the *Ottawa* crew lists, wage rates did not rise overall – there was very little inflation in the Victorian age.

Within a single voyage, rates paid to crew members varied, perhaps because of their qualifications and experience, or because the shipping agent or boarding house master who was working for them secured a better rate. Men who joined at the last minute to replace crew who had not shown up or been discharged sick often commanded higher rates also, so clearly wages were open to negotiation. Furthermore long-serving crew members received what we might call a 'loyalty bonus'. The wages of the faithful mate William Bunker rose steadily from £5 10s to £7 over an eleven year period (while average crew earnings did not alter overall), and the steward John Willcocks, who started on £3 7s 6d in 1864, was receiving £5 10s per month by 1875 (though his wage rate fell again on his last two voyages).

In addition to receiving a monthly sum, seamen were often allocated an advance equal to one month's wages, which might be used as a credit note for ale or other goods before coming on board, but which would often go to the crimp or boarding house master as his fee. However this could only be redeemed when the ship and seaman returned safe to port at the end of the voyage, so if the seaman deserted or the ship foundered the advance was lost. Crew lists often also note how much the sailor can receive as a monthly allowance, often half the monthly wages, which was paid out at the Master's discretion when the ship was in port or at sea.

The balance of wages that seamen brought back varied according to how profligate or otherwise the individual was, and after a long voyage with less opportunity for spending some men could receive quite a tidy sum: for instance in 1869 after a four month voyage to Quebec, the carpenter, who on this occasion was paid only £4 10s a month, had a balance of £10 11s 9d, which we might consider equivalent to approximately £5,390 today.

Take-home pay was then, as now, subject to various deductions, which included the agreed advance, and a shipping fee of 1s. In 1881, arriving back in North Shields after a year at sea visiting Rio and Burma, AB John Walker, who was paid £2 10s a month, and the same as an advance, was given £1 3s 2d for his train ticket to Lower Hill, London, and a cash advance of £1. There were £22 4s 9d deductions on the ship's books, which would include shipping fee, the £2 10s advance, plus goods such as tobacco and soap which might be purchased on board and any money given as an allowance to spend in port, so that on arriving back at the Shipping Office at London South Hill, he received £6 8s 7d (perhaps £2,740 today).

Wage rates fluctuated, but generally tended to be lower for voyages starting in the winter months, or early Spring, perhaps because there were more men available to hire. Wages to American destinations – especially Boston or Pensacola – tended to be higher overall, and rates for sailings later in the summer and autumn were better too. Also individual Masters clearly had an influence, as Dunn generally paid more to his seamen, and saw fewer desertions as a consequence.

Where replacement seamen had to be taken on in foreign ports to fill places left empty by desertion or sickness, wage rates varied also. Some such as Cape Verde paid no more than British ports, in Moulmein sailors were paid only a few shillings more, but US ports and especially Quebec offered very good rates, hence the high rates of desertions there. Seamen could get as much as £6 per month at Pensacola, and the same from Quebec, rising as high as £10 for Autumn sailings, as the pressure to sail before the port iced up in November sent rates soaring. Despite bonuses paid to crimps, a seaman sailing from Quebec could receive the same balance of wages at the end of the voyage as one who had done the journey there and back from a British port, which could not have made him popular! Sometimes, despite the higher rate at which they were taken on, men finished badly off, as the passage from Quebec to British ports frequently took less than a month, and the crimp who organised his berth would take a high cut. For instance in 1877 John McGregor, a Scotsman, was taken on there at £6 per month, but he only received £1 as the balance of wages when he arrived in Barrow.

1881

The vessel arrived in Plymouth on 5th January on an evening when the wind was fresh and the weather fine. In February she had a major overhaul, the felt and yellow metal on her hull were renewed, and she had her next Special Survey, which was due. This time the repairs must have been carried out well, as her status of A1 5 was restored[13]. She set out for Cardiff on March 2nd, arriving on 5th and sailing, no doubt with coal, for Rio, with George Barrett, brother of John, as Bosun. This was to be the last voyage on the *Ottawa* for the drink-loving and sometimes troublesome steward, John Willcocks. A 16-year-old boy was hired as assistant for him, but the lad never joined. The *Ottawa* arrived in Rio on 25th May and from there sailed on June 29th, heading eastwards across the South Atlantic for Moulmein, where she arrived on 5th September after a passage of two months. Before she left on 8th October, one man deserted, one of the few men who skipped ship in that port.

1882

By March 6th the vessel was seen off Plymouth, arriving at North Shields on 11th March, so clearly this time the winds in the Channel were favourable. The crew were discharged there, and the Ship's Articles record the payments made to some of the crew, which show that they were given their fare to their port of choice, together sometimes with £1 cash advance, and a note for their balance of pay redeemable at their destination: London South Hill and Cardiff are both mentioned. Here George Barrett left the ship, and I have not been able to discover anything of his subsequent history. For his part, John Willcocks left also with £34 towards his retirement. He was now 63, which was a very good age for a sailor, although he was claiming to be 57 on the crew list. His first grandson was born early the same year, and was named John after his two grandfathers, and Crocker (his mother's maiden name), and perhaps this influenced John Senior's decision to leave. His granddaughter Mary was born the next year. I have not been able to find his death certificate, and it is just possible that the call of the sea was too strong for him, and he was the John Willcocks, steward on board the steamship Avia, who died of yellow fever at Bahia on 14th April 1894. In that case he was claiming to be 60, although he would in fact have been a few days off 74!

By May 17th the *Ottawa* had gone on to Cardiff, 'carrying timber' according to the Western Mail, but this must have surely been an error, and she was probably in ballast[14]. She was cleared on 12th June for Cape Verde Islands, no doubt with coal, arriving 11th July, where James McAndrew, AB, a Liverpudlian, was imprisoned by a naval court for 12 weeks and his wages forfeited. The ship went on to Pensacola arriving 27th October after again being quarantined, and sailing 16th November for Southampton, where she arrived 31st December. She was carrying a passenger, one Robert Holman who had been a seaman on the *Rhoda* and was being sent home 'under order in the form C16'. Unfortunately a search of the Merchant Navy records at the National Archives have failed to turn up the significance of 'form C16', and this was confirmed for me by Janet Dempsey as follows[15], "I have spent considerable time trying to research the workings of the RGSS (Register of Ships and Seamen) in the 19th century and have never come across a list of the forms they used. Bearing in mind the amount of times the RGSS changed its record keeping practices it is likely that these forms were also often changed." So the faults or otherwise of Robert Holman remain a mystery.

Wages were slightly raised again this passage, to £3, but this did not prevent five desertions. Six men were taken on at Pensacola to make up the numbers at £6, but were allocated an advance of £8 6s 8d. This was actually more than they earned on a journey of just over a month, and they ended up in debt, the advance being payable to the crimps who secured them the berth. They all absconded on arrival in Southampton, fearing that they would be called on to pay what they owed, an occasion on which seamen suffered from an encounter with unscrupulous crimps and boarding house keepers.

1883–4

The *Ottawa* sailed on February 6th for Plymouth, then set off back to Pensacola on 11th. She arrived on 24th April, and took a month to load 266 pieces hewn timber, 366 pieces sawn timber and 643 pieces deals for Robinson Dunn and Co. On this passage the crew were paid 1s until 28th February, then

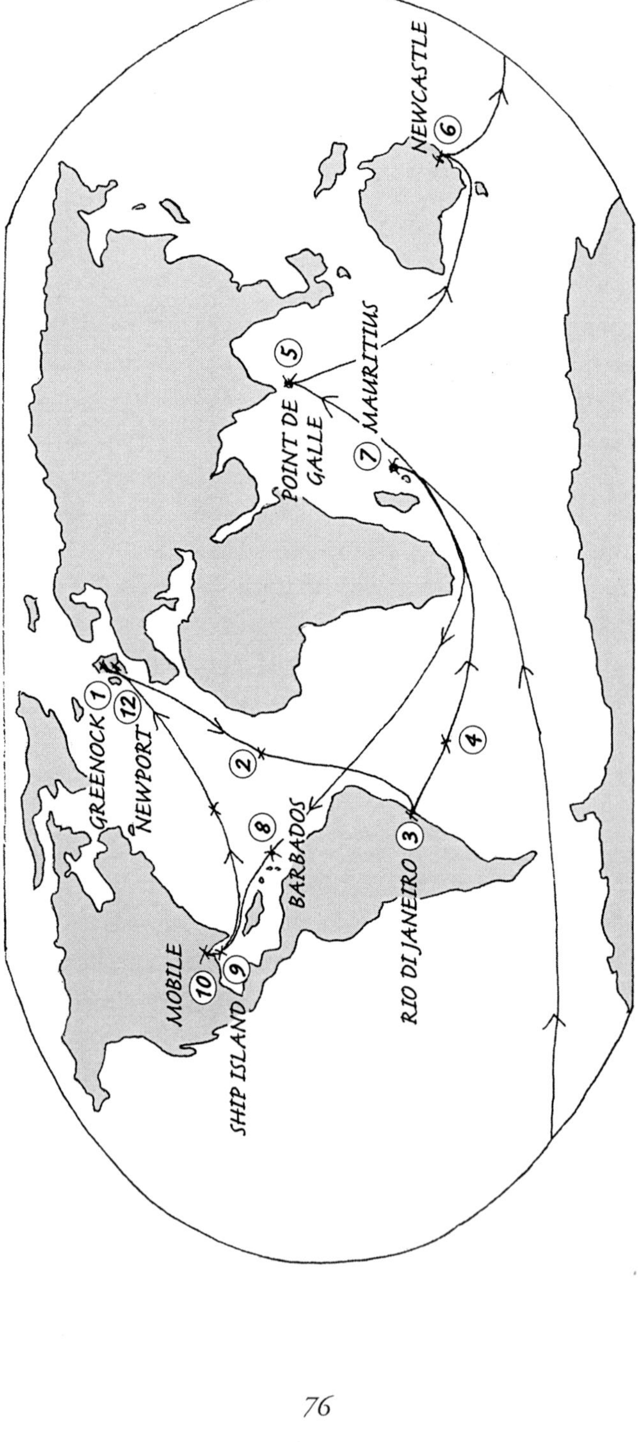
NEWCASTLE
6
5
MAURITIUS
POINT DE
GALLE
7
GREENOCK
1
12
NEWPORT
2
4
8
BARBADOS
3
RIO DI JANEIRO
MOBILE
10
9
SHIP ISLAND

Life of a Ship: Middle Years

Figure 7 (facing page): Map of the *Ottawa*'s longest voyage, 1883/4

1. Greenock, Scotland, departed 22nd August 1883, 1,075 tons coal, 150 tons pig iron
2. 18th September
3. Rio di Janeiro, arrived 28th October, departed 6th December
4. 15th December
5. Point de Galle, arrived 14th February 1884, departed 17th March
6. Newcastle, Australia, arrived 7th May damaged, departed 10th December, 1,315 tons coal
7. Mauritius, arrived 23rd February 1885, departed 3rd April
8. Barbados, arrived 8th June, departed 18th June
9. Ship Island, arrived 15th July
10. Mobile, departed 16th August with wood
11. 23rd October, storm at sea
12. Newport, arrived 26th October

£3 a month thereafter. Perhaps put off by this labyrinthine accounting, five men 'failed to join' the ship, but none deserted at Pensacola this time. The *Ottawa* got back to Greenock on July 19th. A full list of the wages due survives, which shows that most of the men were given their train fare to Leith on arriving at Greenock, with 20s advance and 2s or 1s cartage, wages payable on arrival at port of destination, which for the majority was Tower Hill London and for one was Southampton (which was where he had embarked). Three were paid off at Greenock. This practice served to increase the instability of the seafaring life. Masters and Owners no doubt were unwilling to pay for seamen to wait around while the ship was refitted and reloaded, despite the potential gains in crew competence and team working that might have been gained by encouraging loyalty. Apart from a few such as Barrett and Dunn, most Masters didn't think like that in those days.

Now the *Ottawa* was about to embark on the longest voyage she was to undertake. She was surveyed and part-felt and yellow-metalled at the beginning of August, entering Victoria Harbour on 6th and sailing for Rio di Janeiro on 22nd with 1075 tons of coal and 150 tons of pig iron, total value £885[16] (a map of this voyage can be found at Figure 7). She arrived at Rio on 28th October, and sailed on 6th December for Point de Galle in Sri Lanka, having got a cargo, no doubt. On March 17th 1884 she went on to Newcastle, New South Wales.

The City of Ottawa

Her course would be due south on the trade winds, then a long curve eastwards at about 36 – 40º south, to pick up the westerlies. Then she may have gone through the Bass Strait north of Tasmania: a lot of ships were lost sailing round the southernmost tip of Australia, the narrow path between King Island in Tasmania and southern Victoria, so the western coast of Victoria became known as the 'Shipwreck Coast'.[17] Alternatively she may have gone south of Tasmania, but then she had to get up the Tasman Sea, which could be very squally. 'Ocean Passages for the World', published in 1895 but based on earlier Admiralty Sailing Directions, says[18], "Sailing vessels bound to Sydney between December and April, when easterly winds are prevalent on the south coast of Australia, should, from about 120º E proceed direct for and round the south end of Tasmania, and thence give a berth of at least 20 or 30 miles to Cape Pillar and the east coast of Tasmania, to avoid the baffling winds and calms inshore". As the *Ottawa* was sailing right at the end of April, Captain Griffin might have gone either way.

Whichever way she went, she arrived on May 7th, damaged[19]. Confidential communications passed between Master and Owner but these have not survived and it has been impossible to find out more details about what happened. Unfortunately the owner John Porter Rogers had just arranged the sale of the *Ottawa* to John Compton of Valparaiso in Chile, an Agent, to be sold abroad, but this fell through, no doubt as a result of the damage the vessel suffered. On 2nd July Rogers himself took out a certificate of sale, which was a license to sell the ship abroad valid for 12 months. Sailing ships were often sent overseas when they became too decrepit: other countries might not have the stringent safety rules that governed British shipping. This is indeed what happened to the *Cutty Sark* herself, which in 1895 was sold to a Portuguese company and renamed the *Ferreira*. Coincidentally it was also at about this time that William Bunker, former Mate, had drowned when the *Wyre* was run down in the Channel.

In the end the *Ottawa* remained in Newcastle to December, perhaps while Rogers got together enough money to pay for repairs. Eventually the damage was made good and the vessel was part felt and yellow-metalled, and surveyed, but from now on she does not seem to have had a classification at all. On December 10th the vessel at last sailed carrying 1315 tons of coal for Mauritius, off Madagascar[20]. There are no recorded sightings on this journey, so it is impossible to say for sure which route the *Ottawa* took.

A Note on Sailing Routes

There were three possible ways to get from New South Wales to Mauritius. In 1888, only four years later, the *Otago*, with the writer Joseph Conrad as Master, went on that same journey and she sailed northwards up the east coast of Australia, through the Torres Strait and westwards on the southeast trade wind across the Indian Ocean. This was a good way for smaller ships to go, requiring cautious navigation through the potentially dangerous channels north of Australia, and watching out for coral reefs in the 'Coral Sea'. But Conrad in the *Otago* sailed in August, towards the end of the Australian winter. The *Ottawa* sailed in December, and according to the Sailing Directions published by the US Government[21], the northwest monsoon starts in that area in December, with winds at their strongest in January and February, and it is also the rainy season with violent thunder and lightning, so it seems unlikely Griffin took his ship that way. So more likely is the route back heading south then westwards round the southern coast of Australia. 'Ocean Passages for the World' says[22], "The southern route is taken from December to April when easterly winds are prevalent on the south coast of Australia. From Sydney vessels should keep in the strength of the southerly current, about 15 – 18 miles off-shore, along the south-east coast of Australia, and thence pass through Bass Strait and direct for Cape Leeuwin, not going to the southward of 40º S. When round Cape Leeuwin stand to the north-west into the SE trade and thence as in the northern route, remembering that this is the hurricane season in the South Indian ocean."

The other alternative is to go southward and eastwards with the wind behind the ship. This is a lot further, but potentially much quicker and although it requires rounding Cape Horn, this is comparatively easy in an easterly direction. Whichever way she went, it took the *Ottawa* a long time, 75 days, to get to Mauritius. The *Otago* took 54 days through the Torres Strait, but it is recorded that in 1919 the barque *Gartneil* took 76 days to get from East to West Australia by taking the southerly route and heading eastwards so it is possible that Griffin went that way. This is the direction portrayed on the map at Figure 7 and if accurate would be the only occasion that the *Ottawa* rounded Cape Horn. Either way Griffin would have to watch out for icebergs, which are found up to 40º south.

1885

Arriving at Mauritius on 23rd February, the *Ottawa* then sailed for Barbados on April 3rd, arriving June 8th, and sailing ten days later for Mobile. By July 15th she had arrived at Ship Island, just out of Mobile, and on August 16th at last sailed for home but the excitements of the voyage were not yet over. She was heading for Newport with a cargo of timber, but on October 23rd encountered strong gales from the South East in the Atlantic Ocean 'rendering it necessary to throw the whole of the deck cargo, about 50 loads, overboard. The vessel afterwards became manageable and proceeded.'[23] Interestingly, a scrambled version of this message appeared in the Daily News of 28th October saying that 'the vessel afterwards became unmanageable and grounded.'[24] The vessel was reported in the Lloyds List to have arrived at Newport (to the new Alexandra Dock) on October 26th[25], but was then reported on December 9th being 'towed by the tug *Stormcock* from Newport, eastward past the Lizard.'[26], probably to over-winter in Plymouth while being repaired. It is unfortunate that no logbook or crew list survives from this voyage as they would have made interesting reading. Furthermore, very little information seems to have been supplied to the Lloyds Register after 1884[27]. The *City of Ottawa* had been at sea for two years, in her longest voyage, and now behaved as a tramp ship, sailing from port to port carrying cargos wherever she might be chartered. This contrasts with her earliest passages, which had been from a British port, to one or sometimes two foreign ones where she had picked up or dropped loads, then back to Britain. The story also shows the danger of carrying deck loads, especially in winter, when stacked logs could come loose during a storm, and roll around the deck unmanageably, making the ship unstable and posing an enormous danger to crew.

These and other dangerous practices had been criticised by Samuel Plimsoll in 1873[28], when he said, "If the centre of weight were too high up … in extreme instances she would roll over altogether and founder. This result is often occasioned by the desperately dangerous practice of deck-loading, a practice which ought to be altogether prohibited from January 1 to March 31, and from October 1 to December 31 each year, and only permitted in summer by special license, as the cargo so loaded not only tends to make her top-heavy … but also greatly impedes the seamen in handling the ship." Throughout the rest of the 19th Century, a series of Merchant Shipping Acts were passed that increasingly regulated dangerous practices, culminating in the Merchant Shipping Act of 1894, still the longest act regulating merchant shipping on the Statute Book[29].

Poor John Porter Rogers must have been finding the *Ottawa* unprofitable judging by his attempts to sell her - he did not even manage to take a full profit from the final cargo.

1886

By May 14th the *Ottawa* was on her way again, being spotted anchored off Penzance in a strong northerly wind, headed to Cardiff in ballast. She arrived at East Bute Dock no doubt to pick up coal again, and sailed for Aspinwall, Panama, on June 11th, arriving at Colon (nearby) on August 3rd. But this was to be one of her most traumatic voyages as exactly one month later the sailmaker Louis Laidez, a 46 year old Frenchman from Calais, died of yellow fever – no wages were due and his effects were destroyed. This was rapidly followed by the death of William Jarman of Bridgwater, 45, the carpenter, on 6th September (the wages due of £6.12.8 were handed over to the Consul, and his effects remained on board), and then two days later by that of the Master, George Griffin (his effects were also retained on board). Yellow fever was endemic in South America following its introduction from Africa (more details of the disease and its treatment in Chapter 10) and it is interesting that the men who died were all officers – the Master, Sailmaker and Carpenter - possibly because they were the ones who went on shore. By what sounds like a huge miscalculation, David D Vinny, 29, of Nassau, AB, and James Williams, 26 of St Helena, OS, had both deserted at Colon on 7th and 20th August respectively, presumably before they realised the presence of the epidemic.

George Griffin was only 36 when he died, and had spent the last 11 years of his life on board the *Ottawa*. Coming from a poor family, he had thrived in his career through a combination of ability and good luck, but at this point his luck had unfortunately run out. He never married and does not seem to have had any living relatives, or to have left a will.

Samuel Lewis, the Mate, took over as Master. The vessel set sail on 22nd September, presumably after a period of quarantine, crossing the Gulf of Mexico for Ship Island, but unfortunately one of the replacement crew taken on at Colon, the 33 year-old Bosun's Assistant, William Gibbons, from Birmingham, died of the same disease at sea on 29th September. The vessel arrived on October 15th at Port Eads, Louisiana (i.e. west of Ship Island), but was towed (north and eastwards) to quarantine in New Orleans without docking.

The quarantine lasted three weeks, and was probably not a pleasant experience. William Lord describes going through this experience in Spain.

The ship was fumigated and sulphur was burnt in the hold. All clothing and bedding must be hung in the smoke, and sometimes the crew had to go through the same process on shore, when they would be shepherded to the smoking area, avoiding contact with the natives, where they must sit in the smoke and heat, while the smell was dreadful. Or sometimes all communications with the shore were cut off, and provisions would be slung on board for them.

The *Ottawa* cleared quarantine on 4th November and sailed for Mobile but by the time she arrived there she had sprung a leak. As vessels aged they commonly became less watertight and started to need regular pumping. Where she actually sprung a leak, as here, she would need constant pumping, which was very hard work, as the *Ottawa* was very likely still to have manual pumps. William Lord records of a similar event that the carpenter would sound the well regularly to monitor water levels[30]. On Canadian vessels there would be two pumps, one on each side of the mainmast, probably with a great flywheel with curved spokes to work them. Experienced sailors would know to avoid ships where the pump bolts were worn[31].

In Mobile three crewmen were discharged by mutual consent, and fourteen others sued in court for discharge. These engaged an Attorney to operate on their behalf, R Inge Smith, who had offices upstairs on the corner of Royal Street and Dauphin Street in Mobile, conveniently close to the docks – in fact most lawyers at that time had upstairs offices along Royal Street[32]. Unfortunately it has not been possible to track down details of the court case but whatever its basis, the upshot was that the men ultimately received the balance of their wages, which, on a monthly wage of £2 10s for ABs, varied from 44.45$ (about £9 16s 4d at the exchange rate of the time) to 5.08$ (£1). Most sums were closer to the bottom of the range than the top. Conversely the two who left by mutual consent, without a costly court case, received 39.72$ (£8 3s 6d) and 30.16$ (£6 4s 4d), which seems to imply that the balance of wages received from the court included the lawyer's fee, which, as the total sum was paid directly to him for distribution, he no doubt wasted no time in deducting. So we might well conclude that none of those who sued came out with much money at the end of it, and some might even have been in debt to the Attorney.

1887

By 1887 the *City of Ottawa* was entering the last part of her life as a merchant vessel, and was no longer in very good trim. She was repaired and surveyed at Mobile, and declared seaworthy but Samuel Lewis had had enough. He had been born in 1848 in Churston Ferrars, a tiny hamlet near Brixham. His father was a thatcher, although by 1861 he was describing himself as 'thatcher and slater', no doubt as new roofing methods took over. Samuel had 3 brothers and 1 sister, and started work by the age of 12 as an apprentice slater. Later on he had a career change and went to sea at 22, sailing for 5 years as Carpenter on the *Coleridge*, then as Bosun on the *Amy*. He took his Only Mate examination at 28 in 1876 (and was married at the same time to Martha who was perhaps his childhood sweetheart, as she was also born in Churston Ferrars). He took his Captain's examination 2 years later, although as part of the documentation submitted for this he also claimed to have been Mate on the *Coleridge*, so it seems he wasn't too good at paperwork either. He continued to sail as Mate, only acting as Master on the *Countess of Devon* from 1881 – 1884, then reverting to Mate again. Perhaps he was happiest in this role, and found the responsibility of Master of the *Ottawa* too much for him, especially in such difficult circumstance. Unfortunately we then lose sight of him. He does not seem to have returned home. He and Martha had had four boys, the first, Samuel, seems to have died in childhood, then came twins, Henry and George, born in 1880, and Bertie, born five years later and so aged only one when his father had last set sail. Martha's elderly, blind mother also formed part of the household. Martha remained in the family home until at least 1901, by which time three of her sons were shipwrights in wood, which implies they shared their fathers' nautical interests. But although Martha calls herself 'head of household', she does not describe herself as 'widowed'. On the other hand there is no record that Samuel Lewis either returned home or sailed again as the Captain's Register lists no further voyages either as Master or Mate. Did he perhaps start a new life in Mobile, while Martha continued to hope that he would come back, or did he too die of yellow fever over there? - no record of his death in America can be traced.

The *Ottawa* finally sailed for Newcastle on 23rd February with a cargo of 1841 pieces of timber, by which time James Robertson had taken over as Master. Robertson was born in Orkney in 1836, so he was already 51. He had received his Captain's Certificate in 1867, and was Master on the *Wyre* when she sunk and Bunker died in 1884 (see Chapter 7). Perhaps he lost his nerve, as he did not sail the next year, then in 1886 took over as Mate on the *Patriot Queen*, sailing to New Richmond in New Brunswick, Canada, and arriving back at Greenock in July. It seems he was then unemployed until J P Rogers engaged him to sail out to Mobile to take over the *Ottawa*, so he was not exactly out of the top drawer of merchant navy Masters. He continued sailing for another three years, to the age of 54.

The vessel arrived at South Shields on 27th April and the next day the death of Griffin and the other men, which had occurred last September, was only now reported in the Northern Echo, and in the Lloyds List. Perhaps it was only now also that the families were notified.

Of seventeen men originally taken on in Cardiff, three had died, two deserted, eight sued for discharge, and three had left by mutual consent. The one crewman who lasted the entire voyage was Isaiah Deacon, a 48 year-old AB from Plymouth, and he received £27 15s 9d, which he richly deserved.

Of nine men taken on in Colon, one died, one seems to have deserted as soon as he set foot on ship, six sued for discharge, and one made it back to North Shields, and that was William Dancy, 28, of Southampton, carpenter, and he claimed £29 11s 2 ½ d. So Deacon and Dancy were among the few men who did well financially from the voyage.

Certainly Rogers the owner evidently had again not made a good profit. On May 25th the license to sell taken out by him nearly three years before was cancelled, no buyer having been found.[33] The vessel was mortgaged to Mary Porter Rogers, either his wife or his mother, and the shares assigned to her, a re-financing deal which implies that John Rogers' affairs were rather rocky. Like the other owners before him, Rogers was finding the *Ottawa* increasingly unprofitable. Although she still largely managed to bring a cargo back, delays were costly, as were incidents where she damaged other ships or suffered damage herself. At about this time Rogers also sold the *Nimrod* to EDB Wieting and it was re-registered to Elsfleth, Germany, near Bremen on the North Sea. By now steam ships were mostly taking over from sailing ships for transporting cargos, and attracting the best crews, as they were quicker, more reliable and less subject to accidents or delays, although they were, of course, more expensive to run. From now on, no Master sailed more than one voyage on the *Ottawa*, and they tended to be more elderly – the writing was on the wall.

---

1 'The Gloucester and Sharpness Canal. An illustrated history', Hugh Conway-Jones, Amberley Publishing plc, 2009
2 Lloyds Registers, 1874–77
3 'Masters Under God' idem
4 Liverpool Mercury October 15th 1878, The British Newspaper Archive (www.britishnewspaperarchive.co.uk)
5 Liverpool Mercury Friday 3 March 1882, The British Newspaper Archive (www.britishnewspaperarchive.co.uk)

6	Personal communication from Dr Timothy Carter, Norwegian Centre for Maritime Medicine, University of Bergen, Norway,
7	Bristol Mercury Monday 21 November 1881, The British Newspaper Archive (www.britishnewspaperarchive.co.uk)
8	Western Daily Press Monday 21 November 1881, The British Newspaper Archive (www.britishnewspaperarchive.co.uk)
9	'Reminiscences of a Liverpool Shipowner, 1850 – 1920', William Bower Forwood, General Books, originally published 1920.
10	Lloyds List 1880 Nov2/39 Plymouth
11	'Masters Under God. Makers of Empire 1816 – 1884' idem
12	Converted using the current exchange rate, according to the 'MeasuringWorth' internet site
13	Lloyds Register, 1880
14	Western Mail 17th May 1882, The British Newspaper Archive (www.britishnewspaperarchive.co.uk)
15	Personal communication to the author
16	Customs, Bills of Entry, Clyde, 1883, Merseyside Maritime Museum
17	Victoria Museum, Australia, website
18	'Ocean Passages for the World', Hydrographic Department of the Admiralty, 1895.
19	Lloyds List, 1884 May 13.35
20	Sydney Morning Herald, 11th December 1884, Trove Newspapers Internet Site
21	'Sailing Directions (enroute): East Coast of Australia and New Zealand', prepared and published by the National Geospatial-Intelligence Agency, Bethesda, Maryland. Publication 127, US Government 2010
22	'Ocean Passages for the World', idem
23	Lloyds List, 1885, October 27/21
24	Daily News 28th October 1885, The British Newspaper Archive (www.britishnewspaperarchive.co.uk)
25	Lloyds List, 1885, October 27/16
26	Lloyds List, 1885, December 9/2
27	From now on the Master's name is given as 'Griffin', even after his death
28	'Our Seamen. An Appeal', Samuel Plimsoll, Virtue and Co, London, 1873, reprinted by Kenneth Mason, Havant, Hampshire
29	'The ship. The life and death of the merchant sailing ship. 1815 – 1965', Basil Greenhill, 1980, Her Majesty's Stationery Office
30	'Reminiscences of a sailor', William R Lord, idem
31	'Masters Under God: Makers of Empire 1816 – 1884' idem
32	'Mobile City Directory, 1885 – 6', available in The Doy Leale McCall Rare Book and Manuscript Library, University of South Alabama
33	Lloyds Register of Registrations, 1863, Plymouth and West Devon Record Office

Plate i: The remains of the *City of Ottawa* in Rhyl harbour

Plate ii: The St Charles River today, from the approximate site of the Gingras yard

Plate iii: A scale model of the *City of Ottawa*, made by carpenter Jeremy Brookes

Plate iv: A scroll figurehead, perhaps similar to that of the *City of Ottawa*

Plate v: The *City of Ottawa* today, showing the 'iron knees' (ignore the shopping trolley to the left, this is not original!)

Plate vi: An original painting of the *City of Ottawa*, made in 1860 to facilitate her first sale.
Reproduced courtesy of the Collection of the Maritime Museum of the Atlantic, Halifax, Nova Scotia, Canada

Plate vii: The Northumberland Arms, once a Seaman's Hostel

Plate viii: A double-front-doored house in North Shields, similar to the one where the Melrose family had an apartment

Plate ix: A modern picture of Gloucester Docks. The vessel shown is of similar dimensions to the *City of Ottawa*, which gives an idea of her size

Plate x: Liverpool Docks: the Albert Dock, which the *City of Ottawa* visited several times

Plate xi: The house where John Barrett grew up, by the water's edge at Stonehouses, Plymouth

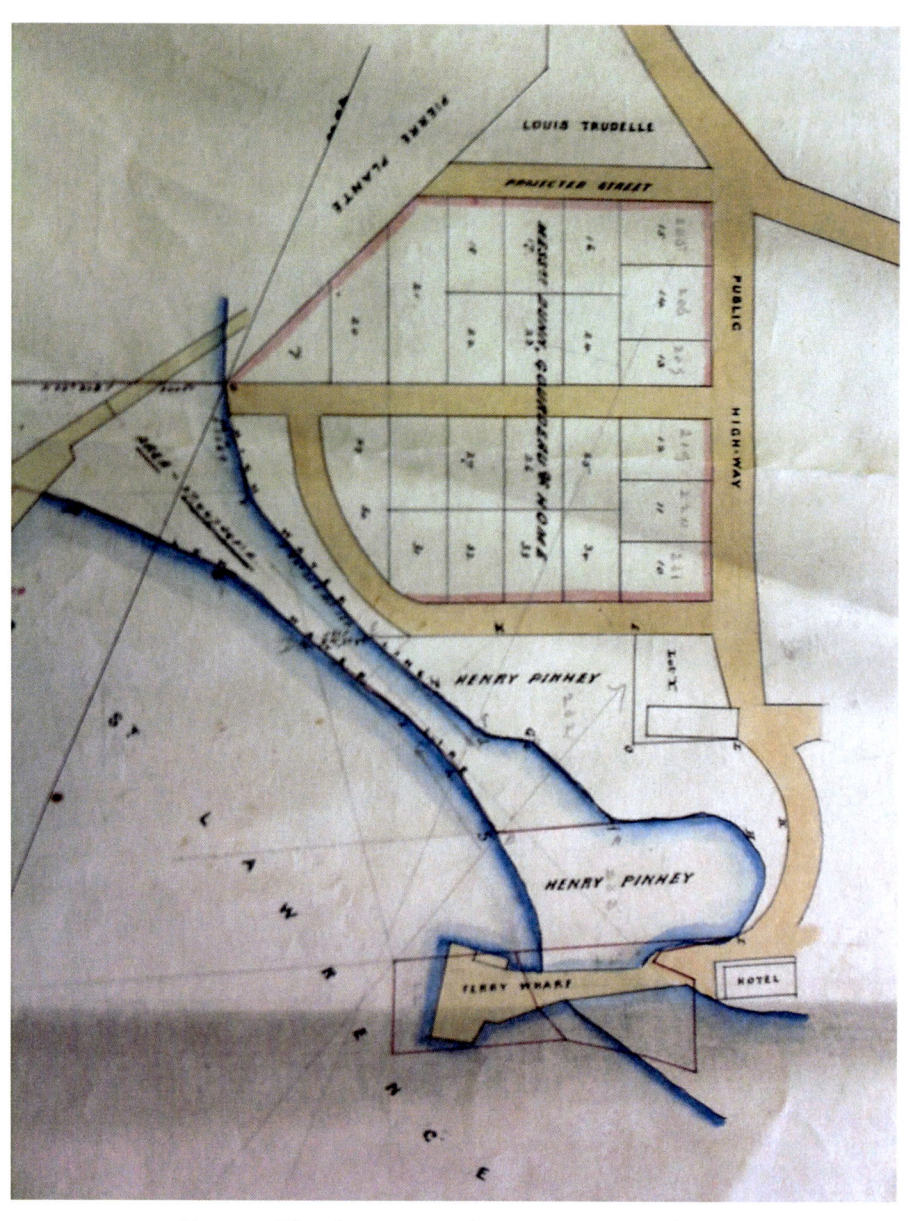

Plate xii: Plan from 1878 showing Henry Pinhey's
riverside plot on the Isle of Orleans, Quebec.
*Reproduced courtesy of the Bibliothèque et Archives nationales du Québec Ref. CA301
Fonds Cour supérieure. District judiciaire de Québec. Greffes d'arpenteurs (Québec) S48
Alexander Sewell (l'arpenteur): E21 S80 SS1 SSS4 PD 088.*

Plates xiii – xv: The three suicide notes left by Henry Pinhey.

Reproduced courtesy of Bibliothèque et Archives nationales du Québec Ref. Enquêtes du Coroner TL31 S26 SS1 Fonds Cour des sessions generals de la paix du district de Québec, Dossier no. 26 1901 No. 26

Plates xvi – xvii: Two of the houses where the Pinhey family had an apartment. The second building (below) is rather less grand than the first.

Chapter 6

LIFE OF A SHIP: OLD AGE AND DECLINE

1888

After a stay of a year in Newcastle, probably while John Porter Rogers sorted out his financial problems, the *City of Ottawa* set off in ballast for Quebec on May 15th with James Melrose as Master, arriving 23rd June. Aged 50, Melrose was another Scotsman, born in Leith, near Edinburgh, to Alex and Isabella, the youngest of five children. His father had died by the time he was 12 and he started as a bookbinder's apprentice, but then moved south to the Newcastle upon Tyne area and was apprenticed to the *Young Dixon* at the age of 14. He took his Mate's Certificate at 27 and his Master's Certificate three years later, aged 30. But although he then took over as Master of the *Victory* (not the famous one!), he often sailed as Mate, and had done so on his last four vessels, so like Robertson he perhaps came relatively cheap. In between he had found time to marry Elizabeth, who was ten years his junior, and they went on to have four children, Jane, James, Jessie and George W. By the time he sailed on the *Ottawa*, James was a seaman also, his daughters were domestic servants but George was a butcher's assistant. His application for a replacement certificate in 1880 showed one of the reasons why paperwork did not survive, 'Previous certificate defaced with ink ship labouring at sea my desk was hove out off its place and broke the ink bottle the contents I found had been absorbed by my certificate and I desire a fresh one'.

The *Ottawa* returned to Liverpool on 16th July with a cargo of 77 pallets oak timber, 111 pallets elm, 473 pallets white pine, 3964 pallets spruce deals, and 1039 pieces of spruce deal ends on behalf of Holme, Wainwright and Co., arriving at the Canada Dock on August 29th. She sailed with only eleven men, dropping to ten when five deserted at Quebec and only four were taken on to replace them. This was a small number of men for sailing a barque. Plimsoll mentions with horror shipowners who sent their full-rigged ships to sea with a crew of only eleven, although barques required less men. Wages were low, £2 17s 6d for an AB but those taken on in Quebec received £6 this time.

A Note on the Port of Quebec

The *City of Ottawa* was not only built in Quebec, she also spent a good part of her working life trading there. The golden age of Quebec shipbuilding started in the 1840s, and 1200 sailing ships were built there between then and 1870[2]. The industry grew as the exports trade increased, first mainly furs, then timber. Britain had an enormous appetite for wood, and huge amounts were exported. Around 1395 sailing ships could be seen loading each year between 1860 and 1867. Quebec was also an important port of entry for immigrants and goods for onward distribution to America and Canada, a British colony up to 1865.

In 1860 around 40 bays were engaged in receiving, preparing and exporting wood for British industry. Logs cut with axes were floated down the river St Lawrence and its tributaries to the bays, strapped together into huge rafts some of which even had sails. Here they might be cut into planks at one of the large sawmills, or exported whole. Increasingly, to cut costs and streamline the business, the whole process was integrated into the hands of large companies.

The industry declined from about 1870 onwards, with the fall in timber exports and the development of ships built of iron and steel. The problems of smaller shipbuilders like Jean-Elie Gingras, builder of the *Ottawa*, were compounded by their lack of capital. Ship construction required the input of a considerable amount of money, which was tied up during their construction, so it was dependent on financing by the big merchant investors like James Gibb Ross. Hence they did not have the means to invest in new technologies and methods, and gradually lost out to British competition. Also, after the river to Montreal was deepened to become suitable for large ships in 1865, the focus increasingly switched to that port, which also had good railway links. Quebec was slow to catch onto this, only getting a station in 1879[3]. The decline of Quebec is reflected in the records of the *Ottawa*, which travelled there up to three times every year between 1863 and 1870, but thereafter visits became less frequent as she brought timber from Burma and the southern USA instead. In her last three years her only destination was again Quebec, perhaps because she was no longer sound enough to sail further. She generally went there in ballast, but sometimes took coal.

Originally a French colony, Quebec became British in 1763, at which point the town was the capital of Canada. The British language and culture started to take over, but after federation in 1865 the balance changed again so that by 1929 French speakers again predominated[4]. The 1901 census records that the Pinhey family was bilingual, and nowadays the city is very French culturally.

James Melrose left the *Ottawa* at Liverpool. He continued to sail although only as Mate on steamers. The 1891 census gives us an interesting social insight into the kind of life a professional merchant sea captain could give his family, as they were then living at 65 Coburg Street in Tynemouth, North Shields. This is a row of terraced houses which are split into two apartments, the upper and lower, each with their own front doors (see Plate viii). In here were living James (when on shore), his wife, his four grownup children, all working, and two lodgers, Alfred Gun, a 21 year old general labourer born in Kent and his wife Margaret from Jarrow.

In 1894 James Melrose was Mate on the *John O'Scott* which sailed to the Baltic that year, then back to Barrow, round the south coast and on November 19th was spotted sailing north past Flamborough Head, near Bridlington, Yorkshire. It seems it was headed up to Newcastle as on 29th Melrose apparently drowned at sea, under what circumstances is not clear. He was aged 56.

Back on the *Ottawa*, Thomas Hellyer Bootyman took over. He came from an old seafaring Plymouth family, for his father John Holson Bootyman, born in 1811, was a Master in the coastal trade who sailed until 1872, and Joseph Bootyman, who was surely his uncle, was born six years later, and was likewise engaged until 1874. Thomas grew up with his mother Julia and six brothers and sisters at 1 Tothill Place, Plymouth, while his father was often absent at sea, and Thomas went to sea himself as 'boy' at 15 in 1870 on his father's ship, the *Rapid*, though he was apparently the only one of his family to follow the tradition. He took his Mate's and Captains exams in 1874, 1876 and 1877, so was a qualified Master by the tender age of 22. The next year he married Elizabeth, born on Jersey on the Channel Islands, who also came from a seafaring family. So she must have known what to expect: in 1881 she was living in Plymouth with her year-old baby at the home of her uncle James Taylor and cousin John (who were both Master Mariners) while Thomas was away at sea. By the time Thomas took over on the *Ottawa* they had had two other children. He had already sailed two voyages to Quebec on the vessel as Mate in 1876 with Dunn as Master, and Griffin as Second Mate, and had been Master of the *Elfrida* for the last ten years.

The crew were engaged on 11th September, setting sail in ballast two days later (there was a light misty sea, smooth at Holyhead). Again the crew numbered only eleven. Once more taking on timber in Quebec, the *Ottawa* left on 3rd November, arriving back at Canada Dock, Liverpool, on December 5th. Thomas Bootyman was to continue to sail, sometimes on sailing ships, sometimes on steamers, to 1911, when he was 56, though in his later years he seemed to suffer an undue quantity of groundings and collisions. Only one of his children, Frederick, survived to adult years, and he gained medals during the First World War as a Royal Navy Artificer Engineer. Thomas lived until 1934, reaching the very respectable age of 79, leaving £2,973 7s 9d to his son, worth £165,000 in terms of purchasing power, or an impressive £720,000 in terms of comparative economic status. He died with his family around him at Plymstock, Devon, of acute bronchitis - which was surely the result of his seafaring life.

The *Ottawa* had again managed a very creditable two voyages for timber in 1888, apparently without incident. In the meantime, she had been sold to "The *City of Ottawa* Sailing Ship Co. Ltd." of 29 Fenchurch Street, London. She was effectively remaining in John Porter Rogers' hands, but he was now protected from personal liability by reason of acting through a limited company.

1889

The survey of March 29th noted that the registered tonnage had been altered from 884 to 838. This was because the way tonnage was estimated had been changed under Section 2 of the Tonnage Act 1889, meaning that the ship was liable to less tax[5]. The registration document was altered, which had the effect of giving us more details of the layout of the vessel. She had a raised quarter deck (which can in fact be detected on the 1860 painting), plus a Master's cabin, sail room and some storage space for the boatswain. But the size of the roundhouse was now reduced, and the crew still had exactly the same provision, 27.91 tons, which shows that unlike some vessels such as the *Cutty Sark* where the crew had moved to the drier, quieter deckhouse, on the *Ottawa* all the men were still packed in the forecastle. There was apparently no separate sleeping accommodation for the Mate or other minor officers.

The vessel was loading coal at Bramley Moore Dock, Liverpool, on April 5th, 6th, 8th, 9th and 10th, and the crew was engaged on 10th, with William James Steven as Master. Steven was aged 44, and had been born at Musselburgh near Edinburgh. He went to sea as an apprentice at the age of 16 and after 4 years was promoted to AB, then rapidly two years later to Mate. He qualified as Captain in 1872 and had been Master of his own ships, sailing all round the world until 1883 when his vessel, the *East*, was wrecked. Perhaps this made him lose his nerve, as after that he sailed as Mate and in 1881 was living at home in Anstruther, Fife, with his wife Helen and two little daughters, Jane aged 4 and Isabella, 2. Like James Melrose he reverted to Master to take over the *Ottawa*, which was cleared through customs on 11th April, sailing on 12th with a cargo of coal for Quebec carried on behalf of Wolf and Powell, and arriving on the 5th June, when the coal was sold at either $3.75 or $3.80[6]. Clearly the vessel was not looking good, as 5/6ths of the crew (apart from the officers) deserted over the next few days. She left on the return journey to Barrow on 27th June 'with a general cargo of timber and deals'[7], but two days later came back as the crew had refused to continue. She had a bad list to starboard, and 7 ft of water in the hold, with the rail nearly touching the water. It is hard to believe that the Master wanted to go on, and it seems he was guilty of at least very bad judgement, if not irresponsibility. Was he drunk – perhaps he had turned to drink since the wreck of the *East*? The owner was sent for, and, while Quebec experienced a heatwave, the vessel was surveyed then placed in Hall's booms on July 3rd, and ordered to discharge the deckload until another survey could be arranged (Hall's booms was where the vessel had loaded for her first voyage, 29 years previously). Between July 3rd and 11th, half the men newly laid on to replace the previous crew deserted or failed to join the ship, even though they were being paid at the good rate of £8 for an AB and £5 for an OS. On 5th the deckload was discharged and straightened, while the arrival of the owner was still awaited. He was expected on 14th, travelling, ironically enough, on a steam ship, the *Parisian*[8]. On 25th July one tier of deckload was re-shipped, ready to sail, and she finally left on August 1st, arriving at Barrow on 29th August after a rapid passage. The voyage could not have been profitable and it was getting hard to make any money from the *Ottawa*.

William Steven went home for the winter, sailing next March on the steamship *Choice* to South America. By 1891 he was again unemployed, but his wife Helen had died and he was living with his sister Ann and her husband William Brown, a builder and house agent, at Pittenweem, Fife, with his two daughters Jane and Isabella and William's two sons, Thomas and George. After that he went back to sailing as Mate on various sailing ships until 1896 when he was 51. By the 1901 Census he had disappeared from the record and must have died, while Isabella was a Ladies Maid with the rich Erskine family in Cambo House, Kingsbarns and Jane was still living with her aunt.

The City of Ottawa

1890

Despite the signs that she was aging, J P Rogers was still determined to run the *Ottawa* and had her surveyed at Barrow on March 31st. Four days later she sailed for Quebec in ballast[9]. This time her Master was Robert Martin, who was 50. He was born in Whitehaven, Cumbria, and started off in the coastal trade: in 1861 he was an unmarried AB on board the *Bee* at Workington, which was close to home, but later started doing long foreign voyages. He took his Master's Certificate in 1868 in Belfast, becoming Master of his own ship in 1870 and had already survived the wreck of two of his ships. He was married to Harriett, an Irishwoman, of Quoile Quay, Downpatrick with at least one child, Catherine Mary, born in Whitehaven on 1st July 1871, who grew up to be a dressmaker.

The *Ottawa* arrived in Quebec on May 24th, and on 25th June was loading at New Liverpool Cove with 164 pieces oak, 781 pieces white pine, 2608 pieces pine deals and 904 pieces pine ends by Smith, Wade and Co[10]. This was to be her last visit. She arrived back at Cardiff, East Bute Dock on 30th July but twelve days later was entered outwards, probably with of coal, for FP Carril[11] and on 20th sailed for Quebec with Martin again. However the Quebec Morning Chronicle on 2nd October announced that she was 'Not coming. – by private letter we learn that the bark *City of Ottawa* which sailed from Cardiff on the 20th August for this port has put back to Milford Haven and will not sail again for Quebec this season.'[12] The Lloyds List reported that she was in port on November 12th. This was the last time she sailed with a commercial cargo.

At this point Martin's knowledge of the coastal trade perhaps came in useful, for instead of putting into Milford Haven Docks (which would be expensive) the *Ottawa* moored further up the channel, around the headland from the pretty village of Hazelbeach.

1891

The crew was discharged, but Martin stayed on to unload the cargo. In April 1891 we get a pleasingly pastoral glimpse of Martin, alone on board except for his daughter Catherine Mary, who was 19 and a dressmaker, and had come to visit him.

By the end of September Martin had left the *Ottawa* and gone over to Appledore to join the *Childers*, a large barque, which was headed in ballast for Glasgow then on to Australia. She sailed on 30th, towed by a tug, but was caught in a gale. In an incident similar to that of the *Carrier Dove* 29 years before, the tug cut herself free to save herself. It seems that again one tug did not have sufficient power to save a large sailing ship in heavy seas. The *Childers* was heading for the rocks on the island outside St Ann's Head when she was rescued by the steam trawler *Dartmouth*, who towed her, ironically enough, into Milford Haven docks (the *Ottawa* was still there, moored off Hazelbeach). The *Childers* remained in the Docks for nine days to October 10th, then was towed out by the *Flying Sportsman*, heading for Glasgow. She left Glasgow on November 28th, but by then it seems Martin had left her, although he continued sailing until 1906, when he was 66.

1892–5

The *Ottawa* remained anchored off Hazelbeach for the next four years. Whatever the problem that caused her to put back into harbour, she was clearly still relatively watertight, or Martin would not have been able to remain on board alone. This was crucial for the next stage of her working life.

1896–7

In January 1896, the *Ottawa*, still 'lying at Pembroke'[13] was sold for £300 to the War Office. She remained at Hazelbeach until June, and on the 19th was sighted passing east of the Lizzard, pulled by the tug *Arcadia*. By June 20th she was going north past North Foreland probably headed for Portland, as she had been purchased by the War Office, and was to be anchored at the naval base there as a government store ship. The first breakwater at Portland had been completed in 1872, but it was necessary to enclose the harbour completely to prevent attack by torpedos, torpedo boats and submarines which represented the cutting edge of modern weaponry at the time. Politically France and Russia were considered to potentially pose a threat so that Portland's position opposite the French naval arsenal at Cherbourg made it of strategic importance, and at this time the Channel squadron, later the Channel Fleet, were based there and carried out manoeuvres regularly in the harbour and at sea. A series of dolphins and nets were installed in 1894 as a temporary step, followed by permanent stone breakwaters, which are still in use today. It was in this context that the *City of Ottawa* was acquired.

An interesting series of letters passed between the War Office and the Admiralty about the siting of the *Ottawa* at Portland[14]. The first letter in the file, dated 30th June 1896, was sent from the War Office to the Queens Harbour Master Portland, through Commander in Chief Portsmouth, and referred to the *Ottawa* rather disrespectfully: ' It is very desirable that no berth available for HM ships should be occupied by this hulk.' On 29th June G Lawson wrote to the Lord Commissioners of the Admiralty on behalf of the Secretary of State for War that 'steps are being taken for the purchase of a hulk for service as a store ship, and it is hoped that it will be available to proceed to the station at the end of July in order that a submarine mining practice may be carried out in September.' Clearly it was already the *Ottawa* that they intended to buy: 'The hulk will probably be of the following dimensions: length 169ft, beam 35ft, and will draw about 13½ft of water forward and 15½ft aft.'

He also asked for advice as to the best place to moor the vessel, and to sanction moorings being laid by the naval authorities in readiness for her arrival – and enquired as to cost. By 17th July a chart showing the proposed position was sent to the Vice Admiral Commanding HM Reserve Fleet (see Figure 8) and on 25th, G Lawson was writing to the Admiralty again that, 'it is now expected that the store ship will proceed to Portland about the middle of August next and as the matter is pressing, the Marquis of Lansdowne requests that the Lord Commissioners may be moved to state whether a temporary position can be assigned to the vessel within a reasonable distance of the Verne and Nothe forts, pending the laying of permanent moorings. I am also to ask if the Lords Commissioners will kindly state whether the vessel should be prepared to swing at moorings or to be moored bow and stern as in the latter case some addition to the present fittings of the vessel will be required.' It was also proposed to 'send to Portland a submarine mining mooring vessel of the 'Miner' type, probably in early September.' The Hydrographer, Henry Vansittart Neale, responded on 31st that it would not be necessary to moor the vessel head and stern.

Costings for permanent moorings at Portland if laid by riggers from Portsmouth had been received by 3rd August:

- for hulk to be used as storeship if of small frigate or corvette type £1582

- for a submarine mining mooring vessel of 'Miner' type £534

On 3rd September the *Ottawa* is named for the first time. G Lawson informs the Admiralty: 'that before incurring the large expense of the permanent moorings for the *City of Ottawa* (the Secretary of State for War) would be glad to ascertain whether considering the temporary nature of the employment of this vessel at Portland she could not be securely moored with her own cables and anchors. The vessel is 169ft long by 33ft beam and will draw about 16ft of water. She is being provided with 225 fathoms of new 1¾ inch chain cable

Life of a Ship: Old Age and Decline

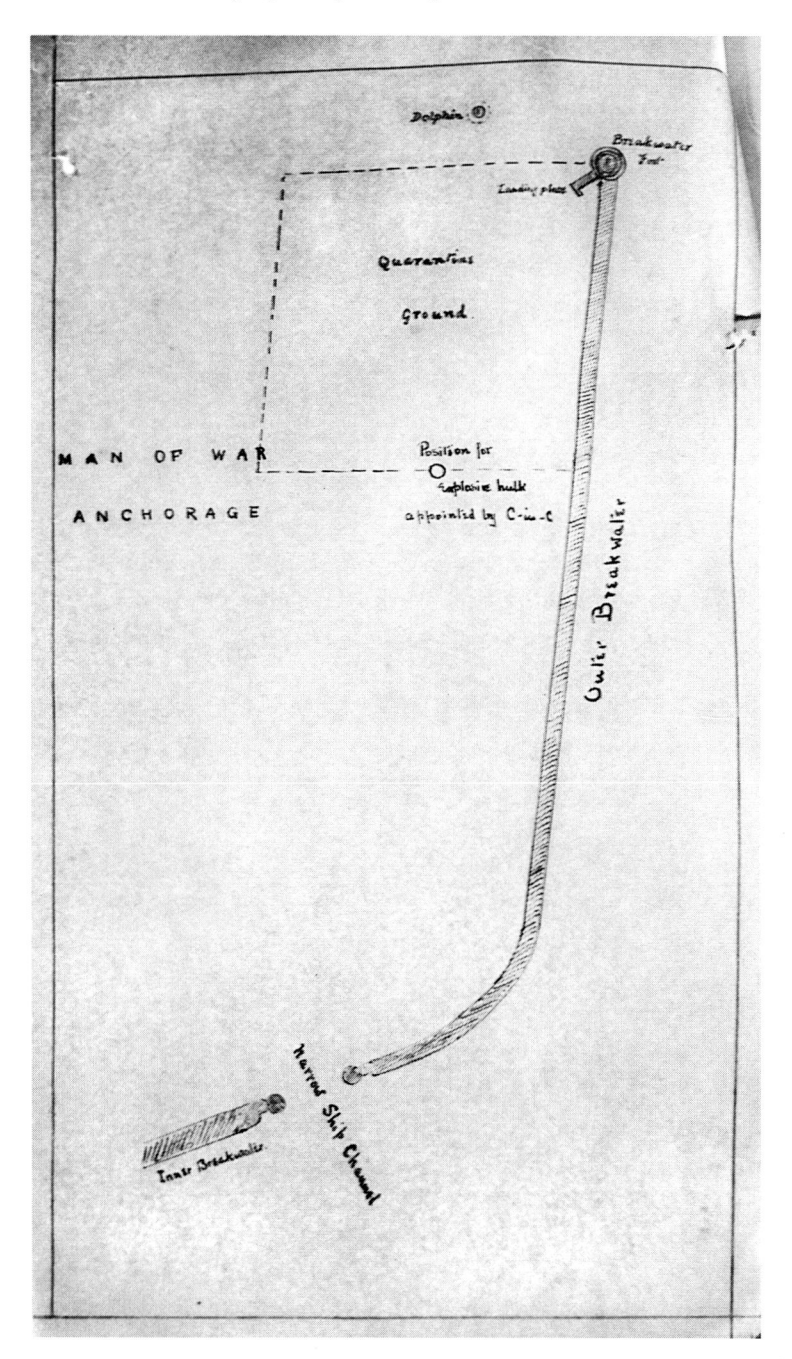

Figure 8: Plan from 1896 showing the proposed position for the
City of Ottawa, identified as 'explosives hulk'.
Image courtesy of the National Archives, ref. ADM1/7279.

and will have in addition 150 fathoms of part worn cable of the same size. She has two 'Trotman' anchors weighing 29 and 25cwt respectively and a third anchor can be supplied if necessary. Should these mooring arrangements be considered sufficient it is desirable that the hulk should on arrival be moored in the permanent position selected by the local authorities.' It is interesting to reflect that she started out in 1860 with three anchors weighing 37, 32 and 5cwt.

The *Ottawa* was being used to store explosives. It is amazing that she was still sufficiently watertight to be used in this way, and strangely moving that even at her advanced age she continued to be of service.

1897 – 1905

Her registration was closed on 16th July 1897, with a note on the registration document that she was dismantled and now used as a hulk[15]. The *Ottawa* was adapted by the addition of cranes and tanks and gave another eight years of useful life, possibly remaining in Portland, or perhaps towed back to Portsmouth as the papers above state that her mooring there was temporary: at any rate she was in Portsmouth by 1906.

1906

By this date she was no longer fit for purpose and the Admiralty decided to dispose of her together with a job lot of other redundant vessels. She was sold at auction on 10th July by Messrs Fuller, Horsey, Sons and Cassell, together with the *Boscawen,* an old navy training ship which was now a hulk, the *Caledonia* and *Formidable,* also ex-training ships, eight cruisers, four gunboats, three drill ships, two special services vessels, two sailing sloops, the Coastguard Watch vessel *Frolic*, and an old hulk named the *Belvedera*. The *Ottawa* was now situated at Portsmouth Dock, and was described thus: 'Lot 11: the storeship *City of Ottawa* 178 feet long, 33 feet 10 inches beam, timber built, metal sheathed and fitted with two cranes, pumps, tanks and cable[16]. As she had previously been rated at 169 feet long, either she was inaccurately measured on this occasion or her timbers had stretched while she was being fitted out with tanks, cranes etc. The total sale realised over £83,000, the third-class cruisers *Tauranga* and *Kataroomba* realised £8,500 each, the *Phoebe* £9,850, and the *Bellona* £7,200. *Boscawen* was sold for £5,800, but the *Ottawa* presumably for rather less[17]. She was bought to be broken up by Robert Jones and Company of Rhyl, and she was towed there by tug. This company had

Life of a Ship: Old Age and Decline

Figure 9: Photograph of the Robert Jones Shipbuilding Yard in Rhyl in 1870
Reproduced courtey of Flintshire Archives, ref: PH/56/261

previously been reputable shipbuilders, but by now had been taken over as a salvage business by a slightly disreputable pair, Captain Hawthorne and Mr Horton, both of whom had had clashes with the law and the Local Council[18].

The previous year, on 7th August 1905, they had bought *HMS Fearless*, an iron and steel ex-navy cruiser which had been towed into the harbour for breaking up, and had stuck on the sandbar in the mouth of the harbour on the way in (as the *Ottawa* was to do) to the great interest of holidaymakers[19] (see Figure 10). By November Captain Hawthorne was in trouble for having taken the cruiser from Holyhead, ignoring an 'arrest' on the salvage claim. Moreover he had lied to the court, causing the owner, one Mr Constant (presumably the middle man who actually purchased the ship from the navy) to be fined £50. Constant was to be repaid the £50, and Hawthorne was to pay costs (which seems like he got off lightly!)[20].

Just over a year after the *Fearless* stuck on the sandbank, it was reported in the local press that the *Ottawa* in her turn had grounded in the mouth of Rhyl harbour, blocking the channel. In those days the course of the river was not fixed, as it is now, and the fluctuating sandbanks in the river mouth were a hazard.

Figure 10: The *Fearless* beached on a sandbank, to the entertainment of holidaymakers.

Figure 11: Rhyl harbour in 1900, just before the *Ottawa* arrived there.
Reproduced courtesy of Flintshire Archives, ref: PH/56/412

Life of a Ship: Old Age and Decline

The Rhyl Journal (which is still in production today) reported on 1st September[21]:

'Another vessel stranded

During the week an old Government store ship, named *City of Ottawa*, which has been brought to Rhyl for breaking up purposes, has been the object of considerable curiosity on the part of both residents and visitors. At the time of writing it is stranded on the Abergele side of the river's mouth, and a favourable tide for refloating it is anxiously awaited, as its position somewhat interferes with the traffic of the harbour.'

However the good news was that:

'The fine weather

The continued beautiful weather helps very much to keep the town full of visitors. The hot rays of the sun are tempered by the cool breezes which make the air of Rhyl so bracing, whilst other seaside resorts are sweltering in the heat. This week the tides have been somewhat high.'

Lloyds List duly reported on September 5th that "The Salvage Association have received the following telegram from Lloyd's agent, dated Rhyl, September 5th, re *City of Ottawa* 'towed safely into harbour last night'."[22] This was just in time, as the Rhyl Journal made clear on September 8th[23]

'The toll bridge in jeopardy

Late on Wednesday night, or during the early hours of yesterday morning, the toll bridge which forms the connecting link between Flintshire and Denbighshire narrowly escaped very serious damage, if not total demolition. Owing to the action of a strong wind and a high tide, a large flat named *Bonny* and a dredging boat broke from their moorings in the harbour and were dashed against the piers of the toll bridge. Eventually the flat was swept under the bridge and landed on the embankment between the Marine Lake and the river, a short distance from the railway viaduct, where it still lies in a battered condition. Despite considerable buffeting against the bridge, the dredger got no further but the crane and other machinery was wrecked. Great as was the damage, it would undoubtedly have been much heavier but for the assistance of a small army of boatmen and workmen employed in the harbour. It was very fortunate that the old Government store ship, which has been brought to Rhyl for breaking-up purposes, and which was stranded outside the harbour for some days, was safely beached alongside the remains of the cruiser *Fearless* before this gale arose.'

The Toll Bridge was the old bridge a little higher than the existing Blue Bridge. The old Toll House on the end of it can still be seen on the West side of the River Clwyd.

The somewhat questionable methods of Hawthorne and Horton got them into trouble in March 1907 when they started blowing up the *Fearless*, causing damage to nearby properties.[24] A year later they bought yet another ex-navy ship, the *Richmond*, an obsolete auxiliary gunboat. No trace of the two metal ships remains, at least above the mud, but of course metal was a valuable commodity, and the cranes, pumps, tanks and cables on the *Ottawa*, together with her copper bolts and other metal fittings, were also soon disposed of.

But wooden vessels were difficult to break up, and were often slowly dismantled and the wood sold for use as gateposts, rafters, door-lintels and firewood[25]. Many of the older cottages in Rhyl may have vessel timber in their construction. It is probable that it became uneconomical to dispose of the rest of her timbers, and when the harbour was reshaped with the building of the new sea wall in 1920, the hulk was left on the East side of the harbour, on the opposite side to the Wood Yard. Possibly she was put by the remains of one of the old piers, now redundant (see Figure 11) as there are signs of a series of large posts on the seaward side of the *Ottawa*'s timbers – these have also been interpreted as part of another salvaged ship[26] lying underneath our vessel.

There she remains today, though at the time of writing new works at the harbour have caused her to become buried deeper in the protecting silt.

1　Application for Master's Certificate, 33023, National Maritime Museum
2　'Grandeur et déclin de la construction navale à Quebec', Jean Benoit, in: 'Cap-au-Diamants: la revue d'histoire du Quebec', no 22, 1990, p 47 – 50
3　'Un havre naturel en eau profonde', from the Quebec port website
4　'Québec: Les régions de Québec', histoire en bref, Marc Vallières, Les Presses de l'Université Laval 2010
5　'Tonnage Measurement, a historical and critical essay', A Van Driel, The Hague Government Printing Office, 1925
　'Hints On The Register Tonnage Of Merchant Ships', B W Blocksidge, 'The Journal of Commerce', Charles Birchall and Sons, 1933

6	Le journal de Quebec, Juin 6 1889 Google Newspapers Online
7	Lloyds Agency: remarks, collisions, shipwrecks, 1889, Banq
8	ibid.
9	The Quebec Morning Chronicle May 26th 1890, Banq database
10	The Quebec Morning Chronicle June 30th 1890, Banq database
11	Western Mail 13th August 1890, The British Newspaper Archive (www.britishnewspaperarchive.co.uk)
12	The Quebec Morning Chronicle, Thursday 2nd October 1890, Banq database
13	Belfast News Letter, 16th January 1896
14	Series of Admiralty Correspondance, ADM1/7279, National Archives
15	Lloyds Register of Registrations, 1863, Plymouth and West Devon Record Office
16	Manchester Courier and Lancashire General Advertiser, Saturday 23 June 1906, The British Newspaper Archive (www.britishnewspaperarchive.co.uk)
17	Western Times Wednesday 11 July 1906, The British Newspaper Archive (www.britishnewspaperarchive.co.uk)
18	'Maritime History of Rhyl and Rhuddlan', D W Harris, Books, Prints and Pictures 1991
19	Manchester Courier and Lancashire General Advertiser, 7th and 9th August 1905, The British Newspaper Archive (www.britishnewspaperarchive.co.uk)
20	Manchester Courier and Lancashire General Advertiser, 7th November 1905, The British Newspaper Archive (www.britishnewspaperarchive.co.uk)
21	The Rhyl Journal, 1st September 1906, Flintshire Record Office
22	Lloyds List 1906 September 5/27
23	The Rhyl Journal, 8th September 1906, Flintshire Record Office
24	'Maritime History of Rhyl and Rhuddlan', idem
25	'The Merchant Sailing Ship: A Photographic History', Basil Greenhill and Ann Giffard, David and Charles, Newton Abbot, 1970
26	'Rhyl Foryd Harbour: a survey of the wreck – *City of Ottawa*', Report No. 14533.R03, Gifford for Denbighshire County Council, July 2008

Chapter 7

Two Masters, One Mate

We can reconstruct in some depth where the *City of Ottawa* went, what she carried, how many leaks and accidents she had. But who were the men who sailed in her? Contemporary records like the Lloyds lists are only really interested in the financial side of things. Photography was still a comparatively new, rare phenomenon, and newspapers did not include photographs until the 1920s. So it takes some digging to find out more about these people, to give us some idea of what their background was, and how they ended up.

Two Masters

Reading the log books of Masters John Barrett and Henry Pinhey, we feel we almost know them, although they contain no personal detail and very little in the way of comment. I was particularly fascinated to find out more about these two men.

John Barrett

John Alfred Barrett was born in November 1830, in Stoke Damerel, Devonport, Devon. As mentioned above, his father, Charles, was a shipwright in the Naval Dockyards, and John grew up in a tiny terraced house at Baker's Place on the opposite bank of the docks. He was the second son, two years behind Charles who was born when his father was 27 and Ann, his mother, 22. He had 4 sisters, Elizabeth, Ann, Mary and Rebecca, and two younger brothers, William and George. George was the baby, born when John was 18 and already at sea. As there was also generally a servant, and/or boarder, the little house must have been very crowded (see Plate xi).

Clearly ships and the sea were a strong influence on the family, as son

Charles grew up to follow in his father's footsteps as shipwright, then 'timber reducer', later to become foreman of shipwrights, and William and George both followed John to sea, sailing with him for a time on the *Ottawa*.

John evidently received a good education, able to read and write and capable of passing the Mate's and Captain's exams. The family must have been reasonably comfortably off to enable this, paying for apprentice's indentures for John and his brother George, although possibly not for William, and employing a servant, the 15-year-old Sarah Butt in 1841, though they also generally had lodgers. And they were by and large a healthy young family, with most of the children surviving to adulthood, although father Charles died in his late 40s and Ann a little later. When John went to sea at 16, he had brown hair, fair complexion and blue eyes, but at that age at any rate no tattoos. He took his Captain's Certificate on 4th February 1857 at Plymouth, at the age of 26 (and presumably his Mate's Certificate before that, but it is missing from the records).

Masters' and Mates' Certificates

From 1845 there was a voluntary system of examinations for Masters and Mates, but when this didn't work well, the Merchant Shipping Act of 1854 made them compulsory[1]. Previously, some Masters could barely read and write, with very little grasp of navigation, although this didn't prevent some from sailing their vessels around the world to great profit. For this reason Masters of great experience and expertise were granted a certificate in the early years without need of examination – Frederick Withycombe was one of these.

A talented seamen might expect to work their way up quite quickly, from 5 years as an indentured apprentice to taking the examination as Second Mate at the age of at least 17, as First Mate from 19, and as Master from 21, with a minimum length of sea time already served. In the case of Barrett and Pinhey, the process took from nine to eleven years, and, for William Dunn, who started as 'Boy', it took fifteen years to become Master. It is sometimes said that seamen progressed through family connections and some no doubt were helped in this way - perhaps John Barrett's father, who was a Naval Shipwright, might have been able to influence his progress. The father of Henry Tiltman, the apprentice, was a Coastguard. But it seems that sometimes seamen could have a successful career solely as a result of their own merit and hard work: Pinhey's father was a grocer of humble origins, Dunn's mother was a widowed pauper, and Samuel Lewis came from a family of thatchers. We quite often see that a good Master, such as

Dunn, would encourage his crew to progress in this way.

The seaman had to sit an examination at an authorised centre, and Candidates generally took about three weeks of private tuition to prepare for it[2], either at their own expense, or perhaps sponsored by another. There was a wide curriculum. Candidates must write a legible hand, understand the first five rules of arithmetic, know how to find the latitude by a star and to preserve the crew in case of wreck, together with a knowledge of lights and signals, prevention of scurvy, invoices, and chartering. The first day's test would be a written paper in navigation, the second day an oral examination in seamanship. Formal records held by the Registrar General of Seamen from the time of joining as an apprentice attested to a candidate's good behaviour[3].

Examinations were held in the Board of Trade Shipping Offices, established under the 1854 Merchant Shipping Act. The Examiners' methods are described by Joseph Conrad, the writer, who was a qualified ship's Master, in 'A Personal Record'[4]: he wrote that the examiner, "kept inscrutably silent for a moment, and then, placing me in a ship of a certain size at sea … ordered me to execute a certain manoeuvre. Before I was half way through it he did some material damage to the ship. Directly I had grappled with the difficulty he caused another to present itself …"

Barrett had already sailed for Restarick as Mate on the *Countess of Loudon*, but on passing he became Master of another Restarick ship, the *Eliza*, sailing mostly to Canada. When Restarick bought the *City of Ottawa* he took over as Master. On that vessel he sailed 13 voyages over 7 years, 6 of them Plymouth/Quebec with a very quick turn around, but also travelling to Genoa, Malaga, Bombay, Boston, Cape Verde and Burma. In his time, there was a lot of continuity in crew, who often stayed on from one boat to the next, and were often from Plymouth and the surrounding area. Of course the ship was new and very seaworthy at that time, but it also implies that Barrett inspired loyalty and we can also see from the crew lists that sometimes he paid the crew a bonus to stay on, to achieve shorter journey times. He didn't have the discipline problems that Pinhey did, but we perhaps get the impression that he was stricter and more ruthless: he seems to have left the *City of Ottawa* in Toulon under something of cloud, after the minor rebellion by the crew over the state of the beef.

In his time on the *Ottawa*, he spent 348 days in British ports, but mostly for quite short periods, when he would be occupied with loading, unloading, laying on men etc. – 8 of these periods were spent in Plymouth. He never married and when in port he stayed, first at 18 Caroline Place South, then at 9 Caroline Place North, with his brother Charles and Charles' wife Fanny. This was a larger, pleasant house above the Naval Barracks, and here they brought up 5 children, including Hannibal, Fanny, Alfred and Amy, though only Alfred survived to adulthood, turning from the sea and becoming an ironmonger's apprentice. Charles' brother George and sister Rebecca also lived with them for part of the time, together with a series of servants and lodgers. Charles lived long enough to retire, and Fanny survived him, to at least the age of 79.

Perhaps the problem with the beef soured John Barrett's relationship with Restarick, as he never sailed on his ships again. After leaving the *Ottawa* in March 1869, he got another command on the *Lily of Devon*, sailing for China in September. He continued to sail continually on various ships, travelling to Canada, the East Indies, and the South Pacific. His last journey was on board the *Ribble*, which left Java on 13th August 1876 with a cargo of sugar, headed for Cork. She reached Queenstown, Ireland on 29th December, and Barrett died there on 5th January 1877, at the age of 47. No cause of death is recorded. However the owners did not let this stand in the way of their profit, as the ship had sailed for Amsterdam by 14th January.

Nevertheless, John had clearly found the seagoing life profitable, for he left his family £450 – which would have a purchasing power of £33,000 today, but as an indicator of economic status is the equivalent of £291,000.

The story of Barrett very much confirms our preconceptions, of the boy from the reasonably comfortably off, lower middle class, semi-professional, maritime-oriented family, who started as a boy apprentice and worked his way up, using his position to forward the careers of his younger siblings. A bachelor working life of some 31 years spent pretty much constantly at sea culminated in death in middle age, still sailing.

Henry Pinhey

It is interesting therefore to compare this with the life of Henry Pinhey. We have more records of Pinhey's life (some key records relating to Barrett are missing), and can reconstruct it in some detail. He was also born in Plymouth, on 14th April 1834, and baptised on 1st May in Charles Parish. His father, also Henry, was described as a labourer when he was born, though by 1838, aged 27, he had become a grocer, and the family moved to the shop at 23 Treville Street, still in Plymouth. His mother Elizabeth had died of consumption when Henry Junior was 4, and Henry grew up in a household which included his brother

John, 3 years younger, Dinah Pinhey, aged 50, probably his grandmother, and a young servant, Ann Hannaford, aged 17. Thus like Barrett he came from a lower middle class background, though from an area with much poverty, with small crowded buildings often occupied by more than one family unit, and with no close link to the sea. His father remarried when Henry was 9, to Mary Ann Kittow, and proceeded to have more sons: the census records are confused, but his brothers certainly included Frederick Thomas, born 20th February 1846, and Frank Albert, born 9th February 1853, both of whom sailed with him on the *City of Ottawa*. His brother John was a silk merchant's assistant in 1851, but others seem to have died as children.

Henry went to sea as an apprentice at the age of 14, on 4th August 1848 and just before his father was declared bankrupt at the end of the year (though this does not seem to have held Henry Senior back, as by 1851 he was trading from 28 Treville Street, still as a grocer, and he seems to have been able to get the £40 or so needed to pay for his son's indenture). Like John Barrett, Henry had received a sufficiently good education to be able to read and write, navigate and pass his exams, and he has a round, backward sloping handwriting, large and clear. He had brown hair, a fair complexion, hazel eyes, no distinguishing marks, and at 14 was described as 'still growing'.

He sailed on the *Melody* for 5 years as Apprentice, becoming Acting Second Mate in August 1853, and being made up to Second Mate in November after taking his Certificate of Competency as Only Mate in Plymouth on 22 Oct 1853. He got a rating of 'very good'. He became Mate on the *Lyra* in July 1854, then continued on the *Nelson, Keturah*, and *Coquette*, when he was reported 'steady and sober'.

He took the Certificate of Competency as Master examination at Plymouth on 21 August 1857, 6 months after Barrett, although he was four years younger. He was then made up to Master of the *Coquette*, then the *Cassandra*, Mate on *Countess of Loudon* (in the Restarick fleet), and Master on *Esterias, Persian* and *Venus*, sailing to Canada, the Mediterranean, West Indies, USA, and South America. While Master of the *Esterias* he received the silver medal from the American Government for services to the shipwrecked seamen of the *Indian Queen*, in March 1861. The Daily News of Plymouth dated May 7th, reported that this was a barque registered at Bath, USA, commanded by Captain Giles. She was sailing from New York to Galway with wheat when she had to be abandoned as she was sinking, but the crew were saved. This information was probably reported to the newspaper by the crew of the *Esterias* herself on docking.

On 17th January 1860 he married Mary Jane Soper, age 21, at Temple, Bristol,

The City of Ottawa

probably just before taking command of the *Esterias*. Mary Jane Soper was born at Totnes, but had moved to Sutton, Plymouth, by 1851. Her father was John Soper, sometimes described as Carrier, or sometimes Greengrocer, and her mother was Sarah. Mary was the third child of seven, aged 21 at the time of her marriage, five years younger than Henry, and received a schooling until at least the age of 11. She does not seem to have sailed with him, as wives sometimes did, but lived at home with her parents. They had a daughter, Alice, born 14th January 1865, but sadly Mary died on 27th February 1869 from cancer of the buttock. She had been ill for at least a year, and Henry had taken the previous year off from sailing to look after her. He was present at her death.

But now Henry seems to have thrown himself into work again, for he took over the *City of Ottawa* in Toulon two months later. At this point he gave his address as 9 Duke Street, the family home of the Soper family, and presumably Alice, who was 4, stayed with her grandparents, although by the age of 6 she was attending a boarding school at 12 St George's Terrace.

Henry sailed 10 voyages with the *City of Ottawa* over the next 5 years, carrying coal and timber. Quebec was his main destination, but he also went to Burma, and Pensacola in the USA.

It was while in Quebec, on 27th August 1873, that Henry married for the second time, to Louisa Adams who was 31 (Henry was 39). Louisa was born in Quebec of William and Ann, the second of 7 children. William was an English-speaking Protestant, who married twice, the second time to June or Jeanne. He originally described himself as Stevedore, but by the time of the marriage had his own business, W C Adams and Son, Coal Merchant. He belonged to the same lower middle class of trades people as the Pinheys: the family generally had at least one servant, and lived in an area with accountants, merchants and shoemakers as neighbours. The courtship must have been a bit of a whirlwind romance, as Henry had been in Quebec twice in 1870, but then did not visit again for two years. When the *City of Ottawa* arrived on 1st August, he managed to stay for a month, and in addition to getting married had to deal with desertion, medical emergencies and a hurricane, so he had quite a busy month!

I have not been able to discover whether Louisa travelled with Henry, but he did not return to Quebec for a year, where he stayed for a month from August 25th 1874, but then returned to Cardiff. That was his last journey on the *City of Ottawa*, and he shortly moved to Canada. Another occurrence that may have influenced his move, besides his marriage, was the death of his father on 17th October 1873, suddenly of apoplexy, at the age of 63. Henry senior's second wife Mary Ann had died in 1860, and by 1871 he was married again, to Harriet. He seems to have had mixed fortunes, for after 1860 he is referred to as 'traveller', 'commission agent' and then 'grocer' again. Possibly Henry junior inherited some money (though there is no record of a will), or perhaps he had made enough from his work as Master Mariner: for the system could be very rewarding to an enterprising Master who invested in his own cargos, as we have seen in the case of John Barrett.

In any case, by May 1875 he was living on the Isle of Orleans with Louisa, just outside Quebec, owner of a steamer, the *Maid of Orleans* which ran between the Island and Champlain Market wharf (below is a copy of the notice that the service was starting).

The Morning Chronicle and Commercial and Shipping Gazette, 12 May 1875

Island of Orleans

The steamer 'Maid of Orleans' will commence running on Thursday, 13th May, as follows:

Thursday, Friday and Saturday next will leave Island Wharf at 8 a.m., will leave Champlain Market Wharf at 2 p.m., returning will leave Island at 6 p.m.

The following week will run one trip a day, leaving Island at 8 a.m. and Quebec at 6 p.m. After which time it is intended to run five trips per day as follows:

Leaving Island	Leaving Quebec
7 a.m.	8 a.m.
9 a.m.	11 a.m.
2 p.m.	3 p.m.
4 p.m.	5 p.m.
6 p.m.	7 p.m.

And on market days, 5 a.m., an extra trip at 6 a.m.

Henry Pinhey Captain May 23rd 1875

The records do not indicate whether Alice went to Canada with her father or stayed in her boarding school, but at any rate she had joined them by 1881, and the Pinheys owned a very pleasant spot by the water's edge in Sainte-Pétronille parish. The surveyor's maps[5] (see Plate xii) indicate that Henry held the beach and land between high and low water in the little bay to the West of the 'Anse du fort' (which incidentally was where the *Columbus* and the *Baron Renfrew*, the remarkable 'raft ships' of Charles Wood, were built in the 1820s[6]). Henry had acquired this at a good time. The first dock had been built in 1855, which had the effect of making the island accessible at all times, as can be seen by the above sailing times, despite the sometimes strong and unreliable tides in the channel. The regular steam ship service had a boosting effect on the local economy, both facilitating travel for residents and ferrying holidaymakers from Quebec, and at about the same time a large concession of land surrounding the quay had been bought by Timothy Dunn, Francis Gourdeau and William How as an investment, for purposes of redevelopment. There was already a hotel there, a four-storey building in the fashion of a two turret castle called Château Bel-Air and owned by Thomas H Lizotte, which was on the site of the present day Auberge La Goéliche. Sainte-Pétronille is a very pretty part of the Isle of Orleans and it had become a fashionable destination on sunny Sunday afternoons in the summer. In some ways it was a victim of its own success, as this article which appeared in Le Journal de Québec in September 1878[7] indicates (my translation):

'For many years there has only been a single steam boat on this line which could be so overloaded that often the passengers' lives were in danger. Many people were deterred from going for a stroll on the Isle on Sunday afternoons because it was so crowded, with not enough seats so some had to stand for the entire journey.

But now two steam boats go there, and judging by what we saw last Sunday, these are hardly going to be enough … Now the owners of the two lines are in competition for the most business, even going so far as providing musical entertainment. Indeed last Sunday the orchestra of the Union Musicale played on board one of them'

Whether Pinhey got fed up of competing for popularity, or whether he lost money overall as the business was seasonal (in winter people walked to the mainland over the Ice Bridges, after the St Lawrence froze each year), or whether it was the call of the sea … For whatever reason, the last notice of the running times of the *Maid of Orleans* was on 13th October 1881[8] and next year the run was taken over by Captain Bolduc in the *Champion*. The surveyor's report indicates that Pinhey still owned the land in 1884 when the whole area was bought by Charles Gideon Beaulieu, probably also as an investment.

So in 1887, at the age of 53, Henry decided to go to sea again and on 27th September he took command of the *Golden Rule*, sailing for Buenos Ayres.

This was a full rigged wooden ship, built in the USA, bigger and older than the *City of Ottawa*, and owned by J Maguire of Quebec. Henry arrived at Buenos Aires on 19th December, then sailed to Paseo (Florida, USA), Le Havre, and then to Cardiff where she arrived on 25th February 1889. He stayed there until September 2nd 1890 (no doubt taking the opportunity to visit family and friends!), then sailed for Montevideo (Uruguay), Mobile and Pensacola (USA), heading for the River Plate (Buenos Aires again), but instead putting into Barbados in August leaking, having jettisoned the deck load, 'and will probably have to discharge her cargo'[9]. The Lloyd's List reported on September 26th that the *Golden Rule* had commenced doing this, 'but the Captain afterwards received a telegram instructing him to stop all proceedings as a special agent was being sent out'[10]. By October 23rd, 'two surveys have been held on the *Golden Rule* and the vessel was recommended to discharge all the tween decks cargo and the vessel is now making no water at all. Surveyors have recommended that the topsides to be caulked and repaired, bowsprit secured and a new rudder put in, they consider that she will then be fit to reload her cargo and proceed to her destination'[11]. The vessel finally sailed on 27th November, but by now another Captain had taken over. It was estimated that the expenses of repair and keeping the ship in port amounted to £1,200.

We do not know whether Henry Pinhey left the vessel because he had got fed up with hanging round in Barbados, or whether he was pushed (the telegram instructing him to wait for a special agent to be sent out perhaps indicates a lack of confidence in his judgement?). Or perhaps he was missing his family and just did not feel it was financially worthwhile. In any case, he returned to Quebec after an absence of three years.

When Henry sailed away, his wife Louisa and daughter Alice had moved into the town of Quebec. No doubt the property on the Isle of Orleans felt a little remote with no man at home. The family seem to have moved constantly between properties over the next few years according to the Annuaire Marcotte de Quebec, from 251 (or 261) Rue St Jean (outside the city walls) to 10 (or 12) St Stanislaus, a very central property opposite Holy Trinity, the Anglican Church in Quebec (see Plate xvi). Both properties comprised more than one family unit: they shared the St Jean property with the Sampson family, who lived there before and during the time the Pinheys were in residence. Clearly Henry did not make the fortune he hoped for from his travels, as on his return he joined the Civil Service on 23rd May 1893, working as a Mechanical Assistant at the Weights and Measures office where he earned 600Ca$ a year[12]. Alice (who never married) was also working (although her occupation is indistinct on the Census form), but she was earning 360Ca$. All of them are recorded as able to read and write, to speak English and French, and to have no disabilities.

Ironically, we find some of the most revealing information about Henry Pinhey on his death, which occurred on 7th May 1901. Here is the notice as it appeared in the Quebec Chronicle[13]:

Drowning Incident

The body of Capt. H Pinhey was found yesterday in the Custom's House Pond about 5 o'clock yesterday morning. As Capt. Poulin with his schooner was entering the Custom House Pond, he noticed a body floating nearby. With the assistance of a couple of men, the body was lifted on to the wharf, and shortly after identified as that of Capt. Henry Pinhey of the Weights and Measures Office, in this city. The remains were transferred to the Morgue, where an inquest was held yesterday afternoon, when a verdict of 'found drowned' was rendered.

The deceased was well and favourably known in this city, where he had resided for a number of years. At one time he owned and was captain of the steamer Maid of Orleans, subsequently entering the Weights and Measures office. For some time past his eyesight has been very bad, and Tuesday afternoon his superior officer sent him to the Great Northern Railway, when probably he mistook his way and fell into the river. Capt. Pinhey was a native of Plymouth, England, and was 65 years of age.

The papers from the Coroner's Inquest[14] tell a different story. This was held the same afternoon as his death (which had the virtue of speed but didn't leave much time for evidence to be collected) because it was initially believed he had been attacked. Louisa's youngest brother James Adams, Coal Merchant, went first and most of the most negative comments came from him, which perhaps implies some animosity:

"I saw him alive for the last time in my office in this city on Friday last. He was then in his usual good health and spirits. On that occasion he asked me if I could manage to lend him some seventy-five dollars which he owed and was anxious to pay. I told him I would arrange the matter for him, and he left quite satisfied. Since about four years his eyesight had become much impaired but nevertheless he could attend to his business and walk about without any aid.

He leaves a wife and a grown up daughter in his former residence No 4 Elgin Street in this city.

Upon hearing of the deceased being found drowned, this morning, I went to see his widow and from the latter I then learned that yesterday afternoon she had left him sleeping on a couch at about two o'clock and that upon her return home after an absence of about three hours and a half he was not at home and that she had thought that he had gone to his office."

There is no mention of Captain Poulin and his schooner, but the body was discovered by Edouard Lacauline, small boat owner, who was strolling round the Louise Basin with a colleague. The doctor, George H Parke, examined the body and found that despite a flesh wound (perhaps caused during a fall) the deceased had died of drowning.

It seems that the previous day he had gone by taxi to the office at 6.30 am as usual. Towards midday he chatted to the messenger, Alfred Moreau, and seemed in his usual good health and sober. He was leaving for his lunch and didn't intend to return in the afternoon. His boss, George Napoléon Guay, Inspector of Weights and Measures, stated that in the afternoon he was due to inspect the weights on the grain elevators on the Louise Basin, which were broken and in need of repair. He also confirmed that Henry had bad eyesight and frequently fell. Evidently after his lunch Henry had a nap, not surprising in an elderly gentleman of 67 years who had got up so early. After that did he start drinking, or just wake up in despair? Anyway it seems he went back to the office and left notes on his desk (see Plates xiii - xv), written on blotting paper, as follows:

'Blind crippled useless and in debt cannot stand the strain' (this is evidently the first one to be written as it shows signs of previous blottings)

'God help my family do something for them I am out of my mind all friends try to help them'

'I hope the government will asist [sic] my family try'

Then he went down to the quay. Did he fall, whether because of bad eyesight or drink or both, or did he deliberately commit suicide? The Coroner's Inquest brought in a verdict of 'death by drowning' and evidently the suicide notes were hushed up from the papers. They were kept with the court documents, where they lie still, which seems a shame as Henry evidently meant them to be read, or why leave them?

What a sad end for a sailor! It is interesting that sailors could very rarely swim, and it seems this applied to Henry – Frederick Lyle and James Melrose also drowned. Henry was evidently well known in the town and well liked, despite the drinking and the debt. One can understand that a man of action who won a medal for heroism in his youth might find it very difficult to be so incapacitated by his bad eyesight and no longer able to hold down his job – an Assistant Inspector of Weights and Measures really needed to see well. And heavy drinking is a recurrent theme amongst retired sea captains.

His funeral followed 2 days later, leaving from his current apartment at 4 Elgin Street, which was not quite as nice a property as those the family had occupied when times were better (see Plate xvii). It was taken by the Rector of Trinity Church on St Stanislas just around the corner. James Adams was present at the burial.

Henry's daughter Alice died on 13th October 1912, aged only 45 and still unmarried. Louisa perhaps then struggled financially as she lived in the hostel of the Young Woman's Christian Association for four years from the age of 76, and died 30th December 1923, aged 83, in Toronto, but her body was brought back to Quebec for burial.

It is instructive to compare the life of Henry Pinhey with that of Barrett. He came from a similar background, and although there was no obvious maritime influence in his family, going to sea would be a recognised career path in Plymouth. He was a family man, marrying twice, caring for his daughter, and promoting the careers of his half-brothers, and those of John Barrett too. He was caring also towards his own crew, and towards the drowning crew of the *Indian Queen* (captains were sometimes motivated to ignore the crew of sinking ships, as delays cost money). Although he initially made money as a Master in the merchant navy (as he had enough money to set himself up with a ferry business), his career shows that later in the century sailing ships were less profitable and he finished his life in debt. But clearly a man of intelligence and initiative could live an interesting, challenging life, and he lived to a good age, despite his unhappy final days.

William and George Barrett and Frederick and Frank Pinhey

The careers of the younger brothers of our two captains are also interesting.

All followed their elder brother to sea, but it is interesting that in the case of each family, it is only the elder seagoing son who rose to be Master. Only one younger sibling, George Barrett, started as an apprentice. The lower middle class families that they came from could only afford an education and the cost of an indenture for one or at most two children. Of the four, only

Frederick passed his Mate's examination. Nevertheless we see that not only did the younger siblings get encouragement from their own elder brother, but the Restarick family was supportive, and we imagine that Pinhey kept a fatherly eye on the Barrett brothers. Having a relative on board helped them to rise quite quickly as high as they were able.

However, a career at sea was not necessarily lucrative, and it seems that only William Barrett married, settled ashore and had a family. Even then he was not as affluent as his elder brothers.

ONE MATE

The other major character who features prominently in the log books is the Mate, William Bunker, who sailed for longer than any other crewmember on board the *City of Ottawa*, except for John Willcocks, the Steward. Unlike John Willcocks, and subsequent Mates, there is not a single reference to him in the logbooks that could be interpreted as a criticism.

William Bunker

William Bunker was Irish, from Boyle, County Roscommon, but later described himself as from Plymouth – it was probably easier to find work. He had light brown hair, fair complexion, light blue eyes, with no distinguishing marks, at least when he first got his seaman's ticket[15]. His family must have been reasonably well off, as he was apprenticed on 29th March 1847, when he claimed to be 14, though he later stated he was born on 29th March 1835 which means he was actually 12 (or he may have been confused about his birth date, as many were in those days). After 5 years apprenticeship, he sailed on the *Rose*, next on the Restarick ships *Princess Royal* as an Able Seaman until 1857, and then as Boatswain on the *Eliza*. Having taken his Only Mate's Certificate on 5th February 1862, he took over as Mate on the *Eliza* in April (with Barrett as Master), then moved over to the *Ottawa* with Barrett in March 1863, as we have seen. Clearly he was a valued crew member, as his wages increased steadily over the period from £5 10s per month in 1863 to £7 in 1874, at a time when average crew wages did not. However he seems to have liked to spend his money, as although he consistently received the highest wages, the balance he came away with at the end of each voyage was by no means the highest. During the 1872 journey to Burma, lasting over a year, he finished up with only 7s, while most of the crew brought home far more! It does not seem he ever married, and perhaps he liked to buy himself nice things, as he was attached to his sailor's chest, as we will see later. But he must have been a popular man and a good Mate, for he is never mentioned in the log books as having problems with the crew, as later Mates sometimes were, and he seems to have had a close relationship with both Barrett and Pinhey.

He sailed as Mate on 14 voyages over 11 years, every passage except Toulon – Quebec in 1869, when we know he was travelling to Plymouth to take his Captain's Certificate. Barrett left the *Ottawa* on March 11th 1869 and he presumably travelled back to Plymouth with him, where he took his Master's Certificate examination on 29th April. Candidates generally spent about three weeks taking private tuition before taking the exam, which fits nicely. We can imagine that the men were friends. He rejoined the *Ottawa* when she returned to Plymouth in August, and sailed with Pinhey for a further seven voyages.

In February 1874 he left the *Ottawa*, to take his own command. He sailed as Master on the *Liverpool* on two voyages that year, to Canada and the USA, but next year returned to being Mate on the *Belmont*, then the *Wimburn*. He was briefly Master again on the *Sarah Bell* in 1882, then returned to being Mate. Perhaps he was a better Mate than he was Master? Or perhaps he was more comfortable in that role. In any case it was as Mate that, fatefully, he joined James Robertson (the same who would later command the *Ottawa*) on board the *Wyre* in 1882 bound for South America.

On December 15th 1883 the *Wyre* left Iquique with a cargo of nitrates, bound for Dundee. By 31st March 1884 she was reported passing Prawle Point and heading up the Channel. There was a light southerly wind, and the weather was fine. At around 2.00 a.m. however, in the middle of the night and 20 miles south of St Catherines, she was violently rammed by the *Augvald*, a Norwegian barque heading from Hamburg to Baltimore with a general cargo. This was one of the most dangerous passages for ships at that time. The *Augvald* damaged her bows and starboard side, and limped into Cowes at 1.42 that afternoon, leaking, but the *Wyre* was not so lucky. This is the account given in the Liverpool Mercury of April 5th 1884:

The Disastrous Collision with a Liverpool Ship

'(The *Wyre*) was proceeding along when another barque suddenly came into collision with her. The vessel rebounded several times, leaving a great breach in the *Wyre*'s bow. For some moments the vessels' rigging were entangled, and in becoming released several of the spars of the other vessel came down on the *Wyre*'s deck. One of these struck the captain, knocking him down, but he immediately rose and went to the fore part of the ship to see what damage his vessel had sustained. He then found that a large hole had been made in the bow, and that the water was flowing in very rapidly. By this time all the crew were on deck, and several were engaged getting out the longboat.'

This is the last we hear of Bunker:

'The Mate, who was given instructions to have the boat put out, wanted to go below for some articles in the locker, but the captain, knowing that the vessel would shortly sink, told him to use all speed in getting the boat launched. The captain with four others got into the dinghy, which had been launched from the stern, intending to go into the other boat later on, as he was afraid his little craft would not be able to weather the heavy sea and the gale. The other boat was subsequently launched, and the last the captain saw of it was just before the Wyre went down. The boat with its occupants (ten in number) was close by the ship, although the captain had previously told them to get clear away as quickly as they could. The barque settled down rapidly by the head, and suddenly disappeared bodily. The vessel was laden with nitrate, the weight of which caused her to sink more rapidly than she otherwise would have done. Only about seven minutes elapsed from the time of being struck until the vessel foundered. The occupants of the little boat could not give any particular of the other members of the crew. They heard no shouts for assistance or cries of distress. They were afraid that the longboat and the ten men were carried under by the suction of the vessel. The little craft, with its five occupants, was drifting about until nearly eight o'clock the next morning, when they were picked up by the steamer *Rivera*, and landed at Dover.'

At first it was hoped that the other men had been picked up by another ship, but they were never found.

Of course, the above account is given by the Captain, and he was clearly being careful to explain how he managed to survive, when so many have his men did not. There is even a hint that he is trying to shift the blame onto the deceased Mate, who reacted too slowly, and was too attached to his sea chest.

The cargo of nitrates was lost, but bits of the ship turned up. On April 3rd she was towed stern first into St Helens by the tug *India*, her bows out, her decks up, and the fore part of the rigging gone. She could not be towed into harbour as her gear mast etc was alongside, and it was necessary to cut this free first, but she was secured with an anchor and chain. A portion of bow was spotted by the tug *Victoria* the same day, and on the 4th the fishing smacks *St*

Helena and *Hiawatha* of Brixham came into Dover with 10 sails salvaged from her sail locker. As late as 24th April the full figurehead of a woman about 4 feet in height and painted white washed ashore at Alderney, also a short piece of plank apparently from the inside of the boat, marked 'Wyre', which enabled it to be identified.

As soon as April 9th, an agent of the Salvage Association had made a report, which noted that everything had been saved that was worth saving, but the vessel was a complete wreck. Arrangements were made for an immediate sale, and proceedings were instituted by the owners against the *Augvald* for the collision. In June the wreck was towed into Cowes for breaking up.

There was a remarkably efficient machine for salvaging what could be salvaged, and selling everything sellable, and it is ironic that so much of the ship survived while so many men did not. The story also highlights what a risky business sailing was, especially sailing up the busy Channel at night, and how even a very experienced seaman could come to a sad end. William Bunker was 49 when he died.

---

1 'The Merchant Sailing Ship: A Photographic History', Basil Greenhill and Ann Giffard. David and Charles, Newton Abbot, 1970

2 'Reminiscences of a sailor', William R Lord, Historical Collection of the British Library, 1894

3 'Masters Under God. Makers of Empire 1816 – 1884' in 'A History of the British Merchant Navy Volume 3', Richard Woodman, The History Press 2009

4 Quoted in 'Joseph Conrad, Master Mariner', Peter Villiers, Seafarer Books, 2006

5 CA301 S48/2 Fonds Cour supérieure, Bibliothèque et Archives nationales du Québec

6 'L'extraordinaire exploit de Charles Wood : le *Columbus* et le *Baron Renfrew*', Eileen Reed Marcil, Les Éditions GID, 2011

7 Quoted in 'À La Proue de L'Île d'Orléans: Le Village de Sainte-Pétronille', Daniel B Guillot and Robert Martel, Les Éditions GID, 2014

8 The Quebec Morning Chronicle, October 13th 1881, Bibliothèque et Archives nationales du Québec database

9 Lloyd's List, August 29th 1890

10 Ibid. September 26th 1890, column 21

11 Ibid. October 23rd 1890, column 19

12 Canadian Civil Service Lists, 1893 – 1900, available on Ancestry.com

13 Quebec Chronicle, 9th May 1901

14 TL31 S26 SS1 Enquêtes du Coroner, Fonds Cour des sessions generals de la paix du district de Québec, Dossier no. 26 1901, Bibliothèque et Archives nationales du Québec

15 Bunker's Seaman's Ticket of 1846 gives his origin as Irish, but it is almost certainly the same 'Thomas Bunker', as it has 'Plymouth' written on in pencil and the next one (with the same seaman's number) of 1853 – 57 gives details that tie in with Bunker's later sailing history, as given in the Captain's Register.

Chapter 8

THE CREW

It has not been possible within the limits of this research project to look into the lives of all the ordinary crewmembers of the *Ottawa*, but using online research tools I have been able to find out quite a lot about some of them, with some interesting results.

We can even deduce what they looked like up to a certain point, although few contemporary photographs have survived. Merchant seamen did not wear a uniform, though they generally seem to have worn a cap. The Seamen's tickets of 1845 – 1854 (now available online) are unique in giving physical information such as hair, eye colour and complexion, although only the oldest crewmembers on the *Ottawa* figure in these records. It is often claimed that seamen in those days were small, but in fact from a study of all crew whose height is recorded over the first ten years, this was not necessarily the case. Nicholas Emery from Malta had the smallest recorded height at 5ft 1½in (he should have been steward on the 1866/67 voyage to Bombay, but in the event did not join the ship), followed by John Betty, the cook who died at sea, at 5ft 2in, and John Willcocks, the drunken steward, at 5ft 3½in. However there are also heights recorded of 5ft 5in, 5ft 6½in, and 5ft 7in, and three seamen were a very respectable 5ft 10in, including Henry Gulliver, born Horwood, Devon on 4 March 1812, cook and steward on the first three recorded voyages. So really seamen were of average height for the period.

Tattoos were common, sported by perhaps half of all sailors, and in the *Ottawa* sample, as you might expect, anchors were a popular motif.

APPRENTICES AND 'BOYS'

Seamen who wanted to get on in their profession, and rise to be Mates or Masters were expected to start as Apprentices on completing their secondary education. They were typically indentured for five years, in order to gain experience and training as seamen. Parents had to pay a premium of around £40[1], quite a large sum, with the intention that the boys could then go on to take their exams and carry on up the career ladder. We have seen that both Barrett and Pinhey completed an apprenticeship. It is sometimes said that the amount of training they received could be variable[2], although as far as we can trace them many of the apprentices who started on the *Ottawa* went on to do well in their profession. They were expected to work hard and do some of the most unpleasant tasks: for instance the youngest apprentice must stow away the cable chain as it was hove in, when the anchor was weighed. This could be a dirty, smelly job, if the chain was covered in mud from the anchorage[3].

On the *Ottawa*, the ages of apprentices range from 14 – 17, and interestingly, they were taken on over two periods, firstly when the vessel passed into the ownership of the Restarick family, and again when taken over by Rogers, periods when training on the vessel must have seemed good value for money. Some apprentices stayed for only one or two voyages, but Charles Henry Baker stayed for four years, and Joseph George Jury sailed on five voyages as apprentice between 1874 and 1876. The latter had been born on 21st April 1857 at East Stonehouse in Plymouth, the last child of his father of the same name and mother Hanna Bella. He had much to live up to, as his father had been a private in the Royal Marines, and told him many stories as a child: how he had fought in the Crimean War and saved the day at the battle of Inkerman by putting his ear to the ground to detect the advance of the enemy army: at the battle of Balaclava he was one of two marines who became separated and fought off 10 Russians with their bare fists, the rifles having run out of ammunition – and many more such stories. Joseph Junior then was apprenticed at 15 and joined the *Ottawa* two years later. When he had worked his apprenticeship he was appointed Second Mate and then Mate over the next two voyages so he must have had the opportunity to take at least his Second Mate's Examination, and have received a good enough training under Pinhey to pass it.

He left the *Ottawa* in July 1877 and by 1881 was leading seaman in the Navy. By 1897 he had left the sea and was working as a coachman when he married Fanny Grace Charles, 11 years younger than him, a widow with two little girls. She was also from a maritime background as her father was a shipwright. From then on Joseph worked at various manual jobs (helped also by his naval pension) while Fanny and in due course her daughters took in laundry. A son was born to them in 1905, and Joseph lived to the age of 82, dying on 24 August 1938 at St Germans Cornwall of a cerebral haemorrhage – so clearly his health had not been damaged by his time at sea. Joseph's life is typical of that of many career seamen in that he settled ashore and married late in life, and that he switched over to the navy after learning his trade in the merchant fleet, which had the benefit of a pension – he was probably quite a catch for a widow with young children.

Some boys' experience was not so happy: Edward Hay Archer deserted at Quebec at the age of 16, while Henry Tiltman was left behind at the age of 17 in hospital in Genoa with Venereal Disease. Archer was on his second passage on the *Ottawa:* on the first there had been five apprentices, and it is recorded that he bought two comforters, a pair of mitts, a pair of shoes, soap, ginger and a bottle of chutney worth in total 19s 4d (the ginger was the most valuable item) when the effects of Nuttle were sold off after the latter's death. On his second voyage he was the only apprentice and perhaps he found this a lonely position to be in. It is quite likely that he died age 25 of dysentery, on board the *Ann Millicent*, in 1873. On the other hand, it seems that Henry Tiltman recovered from his illness, and went on to have a long and successful life, as mentioned above.

Young men could alternatively be taken on as 'boys' from as young as 11, although the youngest taken on the *Ottawa* was 16. Unlike apprentices, who were unpaid, they received wages, and their family did not have to find the money for their indentures. They then worked as Ordinary Seamen for approximately 5 years while they learned their trade, before becoming an Able Seaman. It was perhaps more difficult to rise to the rank of Mate and beyond, but by no means impossible, as can be seen from the career of William Dunn, who started as 'boy'.

Ordinary Seamen and Able Seamen

There were two ranks of seamen, who received different levels of pay. Working as an Able Seaman (AB) required a high level of skill and knowledge, as well as fitness and resilience. At sea in a wooden ship, one of the most dangerous places to be, the lives of all depended on the skill of each, but these skills were often not acknowledged in the press of the day, which tended to characterise seamen as drunken vagrants (and certainly, as we shall see, some of the *Ottawa* crewmembers could behave badly!). The Log Books indicate that Pinhey generally tested the competency of his new seamen a day or two out of port, and if they did not have sufficient skill as an AB, demoted them to Ordinary Seaman (OS) for less pay. For instance on 9th May 1872, two days out at sea and having just taken him on at Genoa, Pinhey found that 'Carl Johan quite unfit for AB in every respect had to turn him from the wheel could not steer shall reduce him to OS at two pounds'.

AGE

The vast majority of seamen were aged between 20 and 30, implying that after a few years at sea and having satisfied their lust for adventure they changed to land-based work, as certainly happened in the case of Samuel, John Willcocks' son. Fewer remained at sea into their 30s, but some stayed on to their 40s and even 50s. The over 40s tended to work as officers, sometimes as steward and/or cook, probably the least taxing of all roles on board ship, followed by carpenter, sail maker, bosun, and indeed Master. Ages stated tended to be approximate, especially amongst those who could not write, but one of the eldest crew members was John Willcocks the Steward, who sailed on the *Ottawa* to the age of 63, and just possibly died at sea on board the Avia, at the age of 74!

COUNTRY OF ORIGIN

Generally, the majority of sailors taken on in British ports would be of British origin. In the early years, with two Masters and an owner who came from Plymouth, a large proportion of the crew came from that town, especially when the vessel sailed from there. But J P Rogers, who bought the *Ottawa* in July 1873, was based in London, and after the Pinhey and Barrett families ceased to form part of the crew, the proportion of Plymouth men was insignificant. British crew generally came from ports, or areas close to the sea, though some came from inland, such as Lancaster, Warwick or Manchester. George Griffin, one of the Masters, was from Wellington, near Taunton, Somerset. Some members of the crew were generally of foreign origin, especially when taken on in foreign ports, and sometimes a majority would be: on the voyage of April to August 1869, the first one with Pinhey as Master, sailing Toulon - Gibraltar - Quebec - Falmouth, there were 7 British crew members and 23 of foreign origin: 5 from Ireland, 3 from Canada, 4 Scandinavians (Denmark, Norway, Sweden), 3 Italians, 2 Jamaicans, and one each from Gibraltar, St Vincent (Cape Verde), Montevideo (Uruguay), Gambia, and the USA. This potentially represents 11 different languages. The voyage apparently passed off without problems, so clearly seamen managed to communicate adequately, at least when sailing the ship. We know from the 1901 Census that Pinhey spoke French.

Most seagoing nations were represented. Canadians usually came from Nova Scotia or New Brunswick. Scandinavians and Irish were probably the most numerous foreign seamen. Other countries represented include Russia, Greece, Brazil, Guyana, Tobago, Nassau, Barbados. Judith Fingard in 'Jack in Port'[4] says that black crewmembers could experience a certain amount of racial discrimination and bullying, and tended to join ships with other black crew, and this is partly born out by the *Ottawa* crew lists: sometimes there is just a single sailor from the West Indies or Africa, but often they travelled in pairs or larger groups. But the ship's destination also plays a part. In February 1880 seven men of West Indian or African origin set out from Cardiff for Rio, giving their country of origin as Barbados, Jamaica, Africa, Santa Cruz/West Indies, Nassau, Grenada and Martinique. Three deserted at Rio, all from the West Indies, and possible Rio represented a convenient stopping off place on their journey home.

SOCIABILITY

Looking in detail at the crew lists, it is interesting how rare it is for men, whether of the same country of origin or not, to have sailed together previously (the previous vessel that a crew member sailed on is listed). Sailing seems to have been a largely solitary occupation, attractive to individualists or loners. While on ship there must have been very little privacy in the crowded crew quarters, yet it does not appear that close and lasting friendships were often forged. Sometimes a small group came across from one ship to another – mostly in minor ports where a smaller pool of recruits was available. On occasion it seems likely that two or three men were deliberately travelling together: for instance on the passage to Quebec in April – July 1877, John and James Chadwick, aged 22 and 34, and both claiming, oddly, to be of Greek origin, came across from the *A Sweeting*. Where two men were from the same country and same previous ship, and signed the register next to each other, we can deduce that they were friends, such as the two from Shetland who went to Quebec in 1873, previously on the *Alice,* or the two Italians on the Quebec passage of 1874, both from *Flower of the Forest*. Sometimes two men who did not travel together previously nevertheless formed a bond on the ship, such as the two Irish boys from Waterford who played up so badly in Quebec in 1874 that Pinhey had them both put in prison until the ship sailed to keep them out of trouble.

Nevertheless when they were fired by a common cause they could unite and work together very effectively to enforce their point of view, as for instance in 1869 over the quality of the beef, in 1886 when fourteen men sued for discharge over conditions on board, or in 1889 when the crew insisted that the badly leaking and listing ship return to port (more details on these below, Chapter 9).

Sailors seem to have been more likely to have had a loyalty to the vessel than to the Master – the Mate Bunker, or Steward John Willcocks both served on the *Ottawa* for a long time, for instance, outlasting the Masters who came and went more quickly - but other officers too might continue for more than one voyage. As we have seen, under John Barrett especially there was quite a lot of continuity of crew.

Under Pinhey there is still a certain number of crew who stayed on from one voyage to the next, but he did have a large number of family members sailing with him, both of his own, and of the Barrett clan. After about 1874 it became quite rare for any of the ordinary crew to continue, and by 1888 there was no longer any continuity at all, with even the Master changing each voyage, as the *Ottawa* became less reliable with age (and also steamships were taking the best crews).

LITERACY

The crew lists also give us an idea of literacy rates, at least as measured by the ability to sign one's name. As a generalisation, about one third of the crews were unable to do this, and this applies equally throughout the whole period, and thoughout all countries of origin. Literacy rates on some voyages are much higher, but on some up to a half had to sign with a cross. Of course, being able to sign one's name does not indicate total literacy, and some signatures are very approximate. It is also interesting that the illiterate steward John Willcocks had his own initials tattooed on his arm – as a means of identification, or to remind himself? Some, even those from a poor background, received quite a good education with a good handwriting. As we will see, John Betty travelled with four books, which implies he was a competent reader.

POSSESSIONS

It is often said that seamen brought little on board with them in the way of personal effects[5]. However there are inventories of the possessions of the two crew members who died on board, and the range of goods they had with them was quite impressive. Of course, both of them were officers and professional sailors, and so rather better paid than the ordinary seaman. William Nuttle was the Bosun, aged 39, married with children, and when he died in January 1867, off the coast of Spain, his effects were all sold to the rest of the crew within two days. His property was carried in his sea chest. The clothes listed included: oil suit and hat, a coat, eight pairs of trousers, including moleskin, serge, blanket, canvas; various jackets, described as monkey, blanket, canvas (four), duck, serge, Crimean; three Guernsey frocks (a dense, knitted overgarment), four collars, and twelve shirts, including four flannel, five cotton and one serge. As underwear, he had eight pairs worsted and one pair cotton stockings, two vests, six pairs drawers, old stockings, also five caps, one felt hat, one sou'wester, three comforters, two pairs mitts, gloves, scarf, one neckerchief, three pairs braces, one necktie, a pair of shoes, two pairs of boots, and one pair of sea boots. Clearly he put a high premium of keeping warm and dry. His bedding comprised three pillows and covers, two blankets, two quilts, one bed (probably made of straw) with tick (mattress cover). We can see that he was careful of his property, as he carried a piece of duck, and patches (for repairs) plus a ditty bag and a ditty box and contents (containing sewing implements), but he kept clean, and was even quite careful of his appearance as he had two bars of soap and two towels, also a handkerchief, a bottle of eau de Cologne and a bottle of hair oil. He was a smoker: he had 6 lbs tobacco and two boxes of cigars. He liked hot food, or maybe he used hot flavouring to disguise the taste; anyway he carried two pieces of ginger, three bottles of chutney, seven bottles of chillies and two bottles of pepper.

He also had three knives, a bag and 10½d in cash. He had been ill on the way home, so perhaps he hadn't been well enough to eat all the chutney or smoke all the tobacco, or perhaps some of it was brought back as presents for his wife and family. The sale of his property realised £22 4s 10d, which added to his backpay made a total of £35 1s 2d, quite a good sum to hand to his next of kin.

The other deceased sailor was John Betty, the 50-year old cook who died of an asthma attack the first time he sailed on the *Ottawa*. He died in November 1873 off the coast of Portugal on the way to Pensacola, quite early in the voyage, so had not managed to collect as much in wages or purchases as Nuttle. His goods were not auctioned off until the next January, and then only a few items were sold. His possessions were carried in two bags, and again we find these were mainly clothes, which included three jackets, ten shirts, seven pairs trousers, one Guernsey, a big coat, three cloth vests, two flannel drawers and two inside flannels (as underwear), a chest protector, one pair of boots and two pairs of slippers but only one pair of socks, four handkerchiefs, a belt and three caps. It seems that he attempted to look smart when on shore, as he had a suit of light clothes, six neckties and a box of paper collars.

As bedding, he had two cotton bed sheets, two pillowcases and pillows, two blankets, two quilts, and a bed.

He had one piece of soap, five towels, and a brush, which shows he did his best to keep clean and tidy, and some evidence of sophistication in a small box containing one ring and sundry small articles, an album (of photos and keepsakes?), and four books. The sale of his property only realised £2 8s as not many items were sold, and he had only accrued sixteen days of back pay, which came to the same amount, so when the advance on his wages was deducted, plus a shipping fee of 1s, that left only 5s to be handed on to his wife. This does not seem much for a professional life spent at sea, but hopefully she also got his ring and books.

It is interesting that bedding was such an important item, and that both men put a premium on having changes of outer clothing, each with a range of different jackets and trousers to suit different climates and conditions. But each had relatively few changes of clean underwear. Washing tended to take place either in port or when the ship was underway with a favourable wind in a warm climate: there are photographs of ships festooned with drying clothes as the seamen all took advantage of the opportunity.

The importance a seaman accorded to his possessions is shown by the case of William Bunker, who as mentioned in the last Chapter delayed, perhaps fatally, in leaving his sinking ship because he wanted to retrieve his sea chest.

It is sometimes said that sailors could be delivered on board drunk, incapable and without any possessions, these having been taken by the unscrupulous boarding house keepers. Perhaps this sometimes happened, but we can find no trace of it in the *Ottawa* record, as it is generally mentioned that those who deserted or were left behind in hospital received their clothes or effects. People seem to have been treated fairly: for instance when Frank Osborne was discharged at St Vincent in May 1870 by mutual consent, after having been as difficult as he could over the past few days, his effects were delivered to him even though he was in debt to the ship. The only instance where someone is mentioned as 'having no effects' was the Italian stowaway who came on board at La Spezia and then shortly fell overboard and drowned.

CONDITIONS

What was life like for the crew on board ship? The Registration document of 1860[6] records that the *City of Ottawa* had a forecastle for crew accommodation, lockers plus a roundhouse. The forecastle was right in the bows of the ship, where half the crew (comprising one watch) would sleep at a time, probably in hammocks. This might have been heated with a coal stove, and besides being crowded, at least in the early days where the crew numbered up to 30, was noisy from the sound of the waves. The individual

The Crew

had little privacy or space, perhaps why his sea chest was so precious to him, and was probably wet for a large part of the time. Rats and cockroaches both thrived in a wooden environment. Generally later in the century crews tended to move to the deckhouse: that is what happened on board the *Cutty Sark*[7]. However changes to the Registration Document following the 1889 Tonnage Act imply that the crew of the *Ottawa* were still sleeping in the forecastle, which measured something like 20ft x 16ft, with a ceiling height of 9ft, the size of a large-ish bedroom, and no separate accommodation is mentioned for the Mate and all other petty officers.

The notice of September and October 1860, when the vessel was first advertised, mentioned also an 'after-cabin fitted complete' (the Master's accommodation in the stern of the vessel) and a deck house[8]. The Master's cabin would at best be fitted out like a prosperous home in the Victorian era with dark wood panelling, brasswork, carpet, chairs, table, mirror, perhaps also a sofa and organ or piano[9]. It no doubt became less smart as the century progressed and the *City of Ottawa* got scruffier. From the post-1889 Registration Document we can deduce that it was approximately 11ft x 12ft with a ceiling height of 9ft, or the size of a small bedroom[10].

The crew were divided into two watches of four hours on and four hours off and work at sea could be relentless, especially when undertaking manoeuvres such as tacking into the wind, which might require both watches at work at the same time. But life on board had its lighter side also. Music figured strongly in the nautical life. Chanties were sung to help men to pull together on the heavier jobs, sometimes with topical choruses. Sometimes when scudding along on a steady wind in temperate seas crew would have little to do and could relax a little, and when work on board was slack a scratch orchestra might get together with improvised instruments. Life in port was also easier as although crew were expected to load and unload cargo and carry out all their usual routine work, they also shared with land labourers a twelve hour working day of 6.00 in the morning to 6.00 at night. After that they might have shore leave[11], which some used as an opportunity to get drunk or find women, while others found more moderate entertainment.

Sunday in port tended to be good for the sailor, as he had a free day. William Lord recounts [12] that on Saturday work would end a couple of hours early so that the deck could be washed and the ship made clean for Sunday. Then the men would go aft and queue up outside the Master's cabin, to go in one by one to be advanced some money in cash from their earnings, with all noted carefully in the Master's accounts. William Lord piously recounts that he and his friends would use this to buy a basket of fruit, but not all were so frugal,

127

of course. He also recounts spending Christmas and New Year in port abroad, when a scratch choir or orchestra would give musical concerts. Sailors tended to prefer sentimental ballads like 'Home Sweet Home'.

Also worthy of note is the tradition of marking a seaman's crossing the Equator for the first time with heavy horseplay, sometimes quite an unpleasant ordeal. Photographs exist of sailors dressed up as King and Queen Neptune in crowns and robes, with much use of rope yarns to make generous beards and wigs. After an interview with Neptune himself, the seaman would be dosed with foul-tasting 'medicine' by the Royal Doctor, be 'shaved' by the Royal Barber and christened by dunking in a pool of seawater in old sail canvas. He might also meet the Royal Policeman, and end up with a line-crossing certificate to celebrate the event which no doubt gave him authorisation to exact the same punishment on the rookies aboard on the next crossing.

This leads on to the other temptations of life on board: misdemeanours, crime, drunkenness ...

---

1 'Square – rigged ships: an introduction', Alan Villiers, National Maritime Museum, 1975
2 'Poor Jack. The perilous history of the merchant seaman', Ronald Hope, Chatham Publishing, London 2001
3 '"Those crimps of hell and goblins damned": the image and reality of Quebec's sailortown bosses', by Judith Fingard, in 'Working men who got wet'. The Maritime History Group, editors R Ommer and G Panting. The Proceedings of the 4th Conf. of the Atlantic Canada Shipping project, Memorial University of Newfoundland 1980
4 'Jack in Port', Judith Fingard, University of Toronto Press 1982
5 'Jack in Port', idem
6 Registration document, Quebec, 4th July 1860, Canadian National Archives
7 'The Log of the Cutty Sark', Basil Lubbock, Brown, Son and Ferguson Ltd, 1994
8 Classified advertisement of sale in the Liverpool Mercury Thursday September 27th 1860, The British Newspaper Archive (www.britishnewspaperarchive.co.uk)
9 'The Evolution of the Wooden Ship', Basil Greenhill, The Blackburn Press, 1988
10 Registration document, 22nd January 1863, Plymouth, Plymouth Record Office
11 'Jack in Port', Judith Fingard, University of Toronto Press 1982
12 'Reminiscences of a sailor', William R Lord, Historical Collection of the British Library 1894

Chapter Nine

CRIME, MISDEMEANOURS AND PUNISHMENT

The records as they relate to various sorts of bad behaviour are equally fascinating.

STOWAWAYS, AND OTHER PASSENGERS

Apart from the unfortunate Italian who fell overboard, stowaways were treated quite humanely, as far as we can tell. In May 1867 two stowaways were discovered on setting sail from Boston, USA. They were John Carney, an illiterate 18 year-old Ordinary Seaman from Liverpool, and Frederick Gartland, 17, also illiterate, a 'landsman' from Manchester, which could be either UK or USA. They were put on the payroll and allowed to work their passage to Quebec. Also put on the payroll was James Pinson, 47, of Martinique, who in 1880 was found after clearing in Rio and shipped as an AB, though he then changed his mind and deserted before the ship set sail. In 1874 a 'lad' called Charles Henry Logan stowed away at Greenock, and was put ashore at Quebec, and although he was never on the ship's register, and so did not receive wages, presumably he was given food and water.

It is interesting that most of these stowaways were put off at Quebec. According to William Lord, stowaways were often headed for the USA, which was perceived as a rich country where a young man could make his fortune, although in fact it was often hard to find work, and they ended up trying to get home again, which was possibly the case of the two stowaways from Boston mentioned above. Hiding onboard could be perilous and on a ship like the *Ottawa*, opportunities to do so were very limited, as it had only one deck, and apart from the crowded crew accommodation, cookhouse and Master's quarters, was essentially a hollow hull holding the maximum amount of cargo. Hiding in the hold was risky as although it was relatively easy to slip aboard in port, this would be battened down when the ship sailed and might not be opened again before the ship arrived at its destination, or the cargo could move and people could be crushed.

As we have seen, the vessel often sailed westwards across the Atlantic in ballast, and it is sometimes said that people wishing to emigrate could book a very cheap but very uncomfortable journey in the empty hold, but this does not seem to have been the case on the *Ottawa*, at least there is no hint of it in any documentation. However passengers were sometimes carried. In 1864 Thomas Brown Restarick, co-owner of the vessel with his father Thomas, was taken from Newport to Genoa. He was 25 at the time, and was entered on the crew list as 'OS' but received no pay. This was only a few months before the family shipowning business passed into his sole control on the death of his father in October, and was the third time (at least) that he had travelled on the family ships. He was perhaps overseeing the cargo, or making trade links. Or perhaps he was just taking a holiday. But he certainly did not travel in the hold. On the second occasion, Robert Holman, formerly on the *Rhoda*, was sent home on the *City of Ottawa* 'under order in the form C16'. He was not entered on the crew list. Was he a criminal, or deserter? I have not managed to identify the form C16. Occasionally also men were taken on as 'working passengers'. For instance in Gibraltar on 23rd May 1869 Henry Pinhey took on two, George Brown from New York, and Nicholas Krough from St Johns, Newfoundland, and the next year Antonio Henriques, a 22 year-old Portuguese man joined at St Vincent. All were heading for Quebec. Although they were put on the Ship's Articles, it was for a nominal sum and they were not paid off at the end. It is not recorded whether they had to pay additionally for their passage, but it was perhaps a potential money-earner for the Master.

ENLISTING AND DESERTING

It is difficult to get a coherent pattern of the movements of seamen: a problem for the British researcher is that most crew lists are now held in Canada and are not online. It would be interesting to follow the working career of individual seamen as they went from ship to ship, but as the archives are structured at present this is not possible. Many more merchant shipping records have been put on line recently, and perhaps in the future such a study will be feasible.

It is sometimes written[1] that, once arrived in port, sailors were at the mercy of the boarding house masters, who lured them from their ships with promises of higher wages elsewhere, took them to their establishments, took all their money off them for women and drink, and when their money ran out dumped them on board the next ship in an alcoholic stupor (pocketing the advance on their wages and sometimes all their effects). The seaman thus lost any wages he might have been owed on the ship he deserted from, lost the advance on his wages taken by the boarding house master, and lost any choice of ship or destination, or even control over when he went back on board, which might turn out to have been after only a couple of days in port. He would discover what ship he was on and where he was bound on sobering up. Moreover William Lord claims that sometimes at the start of a voyage nearly everyone on board would be drunk, and the vessel would be taken out to the approaches to the port and anchored, long enough for the crew to sober up, be mustered, and make everything ship shape.

How far does the *City of Ottawa* confirm or contradict this?

We discuss the first point below, but with regard to William Lord's claim, the *Ottawa* sometimes spent a while after clearing before she actually sailed: for instance in June 1879 the vessel took four days after being cleared outwards from Liverpool Docks before she left for Pensacola. However these can generally be related to bad weather conditions, in this case a gale warning which was in force in Western ports. The vessel generally proceeded immediately out to sea on leaving port. Seamanship was a highly skilled profession. On setting sail the ship would be towed by a pilot ship to the outer limits of the port, but then would have to smartly set sail and continue as the weather and tides required. This would hardly have been feasible with a drunken insensible crew.

In fact the only time drunkenness at the time the ship set sail is mentioned is in the case of Robert Purves, who in 1897 joined the ship incapable and then just became sicker rather than sobering up. What is perhaps most interesting is that the 'joining drunk' bit does not give rise to comment, just the 'not sobering up' bit.

Signing on

In 1854 the various Acts regulating shipping were consolidated under the new Merchant Shipping Act. Board of Trade shipping offices were set up in major ports, where Shipping Masters presided over the formal contractual duty of signing onto a ship's articles, which all crew had to perform[2]. The crew lists of the *Ottawa* show that seamen were generally required to sign on a day or two before they actually came on board, and were often brought out by boat to join the ship: for instance on the 1870 voyage to Quebec, most of the men left at 8 a.m. on August 8th by steam boat from Plymouth to Truro to join the ship, arriving on board at 5 in the evening. On the 9th, four more turned up between 7 and 11 in the evening, but two men were still on shore, coming on board on the 10th, while another, George Ironsides, never turned up at all. In fact it was quite common for crew to sign up then 'fail to come aboard', generally about one or two per voyage. In the Liverpool Mercury of September 11th 1888 there was a notice of ships engaging crews. 'The crews of the following vessels will sign articles this day, Thursday September 11th, at the Board of Trade Shipping Offices, General Office, Canning Place, Brocklebank Dock (Liverpool) to Sydney CB (Cape Breton, Nova Scotia) at 10.00 a.m.'. Experienced sailors knew what to look for before enrolling on a ship's register: studding sails (extra sails added on to widen the amount of sail available in light winds) were hard work, and he would look for studding sail boom irons in the yards, which would indicate they were often used, and also whether pump bolts were bright and worn, which showed that the ship was leaky, and required a lot of pumping, also very hard work[3]. All this indicates that the seaman could exercise quite a lot of free will over which ship he joined.

Shipping Masters, Crimps and Coercion

Even so, we sometimes can pick up a hint that there has been coercion. For instance, on setting out for Burma in 1872, the *Ottawa* left London Docks on January 20th at 9 a.m. and was towed by a tug to Gravesend, where she moored at 4 p.m. By 10 o'clock the next morning, it was discovered that two men, Walter Walgave and Michael Develyn had deserted, and Captain Pinhey had to go ashore and ship other men in their place. Develyn was a 27 year old Irishman from Belfast, while Walgave was 28, and from Whitby, both were ABs and both had previously sailed on the *Inverallen*. It is possible to believe that they were shipped aboard drunk by a boarding house master, and when they sobered up later that night, decided to slip back ashore. It is not recorded in the log book how they managed that: did they steal the ship's boat? Seamen could rarely swim. Sometimes also the Master had no choice but to rely on an agent (or boarding house master) to ship men, as for instance on March 7th, 1867 when the ship was setting out from Liverpool and one Owen Kelly had failed to turn up on the ship for duty. Captain Barrett arranged to have James Williamson shipped aboard in his place while the vessel was being towed down the Mersey by a steamboat. Sometimes the Master was more proactive: on March 21 1870 in Cardiff, wrote Captain Pinhey, 'crew all joined the ship except James Greer whom I found and brought on board that evening'. We can imagine him scouring the gin palaces and ale houses for his missing crew member.

Crimps and Quebec

Quebec was particularly notorious for desertions, and the power of the 'crimps', and this can be seen in the *Ottawa* records. The port was only open from May to November, being frozen for the rest of the year, so there was only a small reserve of sailors over-wintering and few sailors who considered this their home port, meaning that they were in short supply and a highly valuable commodity to the entrepreneur. All ships who stayed there moored in the river or in coves nearby, which were impossible to police, and even though a River Police Force had been in existence since 1838, it was not very effective. Crimps took advantage of this by sometimes rowing out to vessels, or even going on board, where they urged or incited men to desert with the promise of much larger wages elsewhere, or were even reported sometimes to take men off by force. In 1869, six men deserted fairly openly from the *Ottawa* in two groups of three, which implies that crimps were in action – where men slip away individually it sounds more like independent decision-making. Replacements were taken on at £10 a month, for the power of the crimps inflated wage rates. The next year when the *Ottawa* arrived in June six more left in a group. Where voyages arrived in the Autumn there were less likely to be deserters, as by then it was the end of the sailing year, and men who did not find a berth would have to overwinter there. These were the years when the crimps were particularly active in Quebec, as the British garrison was leaving, having granted Canada Dominion status in 1867. The Seaman's Act of 1873 by the new federal government put an end to some of their most outrageous behaviour[4].

Despite the inducements to leave, it was generally only a small number of seamen who did so, showing that the seafarer was more in control of his own career path than he is sometimes given credit for. Certainly when a sailor came to port he could, as we can see from the *Ottawa*'s records, have quite a lot of money in his pocket which if he was unmarried he may well have felt was burning a hole there, and no doubt there were no shortage of people around who were happy to help him spend it. Where the sailor fell into the hands of the crimp or boarding house keeper, he may well have felt he got a good deal, with shore leave plus the attendant possibility of women and alcohol until his money ran out (and clearly some sailors took advantage of both, as the high levels of VD reported show). And the crimp was motivated to find the best wages for him, so even though the crimp would take a cut, the sailor often ended up with more money in his pocket at the other end than if he had stayed with his original ship – though again sometimes despite the high wages he ended up with very little[5]. If the system was so injurious to him the seaman would have to be really stupid to fall for the same thing twice.

The personal effects left by William Nuttle show that a career seamen could be highly provident and responsible; many seamen were married with children and there is no reason to suppose that they did not immediately return to them when in the home port to add their earnings to the family purse.

Causes of Desertion

The *Ottawa* records also give interesting data on desertion – who deserted and what their reasons might have been. On eighteen out of thirty-four voyages, or on over half of them, nobody deserted at all. Sometimes only one or two deserted, sometimes several slipped away singly or, rarely, in pairs (confirming that seamen were generally loners), sometimes men deserted in what seems to be a coordinated group. The majority of deserters were ABs, in their mid to late 20s and 30s, with a few in their 40s or still in their teens (when they were likely to still be an OS), and also occasionally a cook, steward or bosun's mate, so it can be supposed that in general they had a bit of experience, and knew what they were doing, whatever their motivations were.

Quite often it looks as though men had deliberately taken the ship with a view to deserting in order to return home, as happened in 1873, when there was only one deserter in Quebec, the 33 year old cook from St John's, New Brunswick. Men who deserted in Rio di Janeiro quite often gave the West Indies as their country of origin and it seems probable that they saw Rio as a convenient stepping off place for the last leg of their journey home, as mentioned above. Often the Norwegians on board jumped ship in Pensacola, which had a very strong Norwegian community. There were clearly countries of choice for deserters – only one man is recorded as deserting in Moulmein, Burma, a 26 year-old AB from Glasgow. On the one occasion when the vessel stopped at Boston, nine deserted, including both of the Irishmen on board (Boston was known as the 'Irish Capital' of the US). America was generally considered to be a land of opportunity.

Sometimes we can see that external pressures may have led to a high incidence of desertions, as in 1873 when seven slipped away at Pensacola. The cook, John Betty, had died suddenly and shockingly when the vessel was a few days out of port in Britain, and this possibly upset the crew, who maybe saw it as an ill omen. In 1880 when four left illicitly in Mobile, the ship was under quarantine, which would have been an unpleasant experience, and possibly the threat of sickness on board made the vessel a dangerous place to be (although there is no record that anyone died, or was left behind in hospital). And in 1889, on the last voyage for which records remain, no less than 18 deserted, but by now the vessel was getting very old. When she first put into Quebec from Liverpool with coal, on 5th June, ten men, or 5/6ths of the crew excluding the officers, deserted the day after arrival. She was loaded with timber, and sailed on 27th June, but put back into port two days later disabled - when four more skipped ship, followed by four more two weeks later. In addition four more who signed up 'failed to join': we imagine they took one look at the vessel and beat a hasty retreat. In this case the desertions were surely caused by the poor state of the vessel.

Being in debt to the ship could be another motive, for instance on September 12th 1870, James Webster was put in prison in Quebec by orders of civil authorities. Two days later Pinhey took him out on payment of the 18s fine (which would have been deducted from his wages), and he showed his gratitude by deserting on the 20th.

The Master and Desertion

It seems the Master often accepted the status quo with regard to deserters, partly in recognition of the difficulty of getting justice against the crimps. Sometimes he might be pleased to get rid of a troublemaker, for instance Thomas Gill whom he accused of stealing canvas. Men who deserted left behind any wages owing, so it did not make financial sense to pursue them unless the man leaving was in debt of a large sum to the ship, or perhaps not even then. When in port, the Master wanted to unload and reload as quickly as possible and get away, so the absence of some of his men meant he had to hire local labour to help in this operation, incurring extra expense, plus seamen hired locally to replace those who had left were likely to demand a higher rate of wages. We see in the records that the Master would sometimes take steps to prevent men from leaving illegitimately, as for instance in 1869, when William Brookes threatened to desert, the Master took his clothes and confined him to the after cabin to sleep off the drink. Sometimes he even went into the port to fetch men back, as in 1874 when John Dwyer and James O'Brian left the ship without leave, and 'the Master met them and drove them on board again'. This was not effective, as they slipped off again, and this time the Master pursuing them, 'met John Dwyer and gave him in charge of Police'. However nothing Pinhey did is as extreme as the action of the next Master,

William Dunn, in the case of John Kelso, an OS aged 20 from San Francisco, who signed up on 21st September 1876 in Quebec, and on 22nd was 'committed to goal for ten weeks for refusing to proceed to sea, no wages due to him'. This sounds very much as if he had been bundled on board by crimps, and on realising where he was, refused to proceed – but 10 weeks in prison seems a harsh penalty.

Leaving legitimately

Seamen also had the option of leaving legitimately. Although when they signed on it was for the duration of the voyage, usually from home port, to port abroad, and back to British port, they quite frequently it seemed could either negotiate for discharge, or go to the courts to sue for it if they had a good case. In fact, the various Masters seem to have been willing to discharge a crew member by mutual consent if he could put up a good case for it: so on August 31st 1868 at noon in Moulmein, Burma, Captain Barrett took Matthew Madden AB, 'wishing to leave the ship', before the Shipping Master and discharged him. And on March 3rd 1866 at Penarth, before the ship had set sail, 'William J Osbourne AB being offered a Mate's situation discharged him before the Cardiff Shipping Master'.

Sometimes the crew had to resort to law to get their freedom from the ship. On the difficult voyage of 1886/7 during which four men died of yellow fever, the ship was held up twice in quarantine and then was found to be leaking, fourteen men, working together, sued for discharge and payment of wages at Mobile, USA, and 'said suit having been settled by libel and compromise, amount of wages due said seamen was paid to R Inge Attorney in fact for the seamen'. It has not been possible to trace further details of the legal case. Grounds for suing for discharge could include non-payment of wages, coercion (if the seaman had been carried on board sick or drunk or drugged) or if they were being paid by the run and the vessel had to spend a long time in port being repaired, or, most commonly of all, an error in the Ship's Articles. There could be many potential irregularities: the absence or alteration of the signatures of the men or the Master, failure to ensure the Articles were read through to the crew or deviation to the voyage as set down. If a crewman was illiterate, the Magistrate was more likely to be lenient in these cases[6]. Presumably the men claimed that it was unreasonable to expect them to continue. They were being paid by the month though may not have received pay while the ship was idle. Unlike deserters, who forfeited any pay owing, they received a considerable sum in back pay, but no doubt had to dispense a proportion of this to the Attorney, and the three further crew members who negotiated a discharge 'by mutual consent' probably ended up better off.

CRIME AND MISDEMEANOURS

Although many things which it would be useful for the modern researcher to know were not recorded in the log, incidents where sailors refused to work or generally kicked against the system are put down in detail, as these entries might have been needed in evidence of disputes over detention of wages, legal cases etc. The most frequently mentioned misdemeanour was being absent without leave, as in November 1867 when Richard Lee AB, Henry John AB, and William Thomas OS slipped from their ship when it was moored in Cardiff, and had two days' pay deducted. Sometimes there would be an epidemic of unauthorised absences and consequent incidents with drunkenness, and it seems some ports were especially popular in this respect, in particular Quebec and La Spezia, Italy. Not infrequently excessive alcohol consumption resulted in abusive language and violence. Sometimes there were incidents of theft, as when Pinhey found Thomas Gill in possession of canvas, or equipment was stolen at La Spezia. Some voyages passed peacefully with little or no wrongdoing, which suggests that it took one or more troublemakers to incite the rest of the crew, and the rate of bad behaviour is clearly linked to the numbers of desertions, as often the troublemakers were the ones who skipped ship.

Seamen were sometimes arrested for something they did while on land: for instance Colin McPherson had to appear at the Police Court at Moulmein, Burma, in July 1871, and was absent all day, from 7 a.m. until 5 p.m., and in April 1872 John Ridley spent five days in jail in La Spezia for insolence and smoking. And James McAndrew was taken before the Naval Court at Cape Verde in August 1882 and imprisoned for 12 weeks, for an unspecified crime committed on shore against the Navy. Generally courts abroad were happy to release the prisoner back to the ship when she sailed, rather than keeping the prisoner at their own expense.

The Police

Although as we have seen the police in Quebec were not effective in dealing with crimps, on occasion they were more proactive: in 1870 in Quebec we have seen that they brought back August Jose, a deserter, in the Police launch. In 1874, on his last voyage before retiring to Quebec, Pinhey worked closely with the police and the judicial system to deal with a particular group of troublemakers. We can see that the courts acted mostly in the interests of the shipowner and Master rather than the sailor, with those attempting to desert or causing a nuisance being quickly confined to jail until the ship sailed. The Seaman's Act of 1873 in fact tightened the system to the advantage of the Master and merchant against the sailor, and it is interesting that it is after this that Pinhey in particular seems to have had much more recourse to calling in the police to enforce discipline. However the process cost him money: Pinhey had to pay expenses of £6.5s to get John Dwyer out of jail, and when Walford was brought on board at Moulmein by the police, the Master had to pay 5 rupees. If a seaman was sent to prison, the Master had to arrange for local labour to work in the missing crewman's place, and the cost of both these things could be deducted from the seaman's pay – unless he absconded first – as happened in the case of James Webster, mentioned above.

A Bad Press

To the inhabitants of a port town, the seaman might seem like a troublemaker, getting drunk, and causing fights[7], especially in a town like Quebec where sailing was squeezed into half the year. It is particularly useful to study the situation in this port, where the *Ottawa* spent a lot of her time, and where the condition of the sailor has been particularly well documented by researchers[8]. The sailor was often typecast in print as drunken, dissolute vagrants, and certainly, as we have seen, some of the *Ottawa* crew did not behave well. Unfortunately violence, arguments, abusive language, tended to be concentrated into the periods when the vessel was in port, partly because of the amount of alcohol imbibed there – when a seaman had an opportunity to drink, he tended to compress all his consumption into the few days that he had access to it, to make up for all the months at sea when he didn't. But also resentments that may have been brewing at sea were held at bay by demanding working practises and discipline, plus the threat perhaps of being put into irons – although the strictest penalties exacted on the *Ottawa* were deducting pay, and confinement to the after cabin to sleep off the effects of the alcohol.

But the seafarer was the outsider and his stay in port towns was likely to be transitory. It was easy to put the worst interpretation on his acts: Judith Fingard says that if found in the street at night he was likely to be arrested as a suspicious malingerer, whereas the reality could quite well be that in the badly or unlit streets of a foreign town he might have merely been lost and trying to get back to his ship. Sailor's misdemeanours were more visible than those of the rest of the population, as justice was dispensed very quickly in the lower courts, because of the short time he was likely to be in port, including more serious crimes which would normally be dealt with in higher courts over a longer period of time. Contemporary writers were often hostile and quick to seize on the mariner as a scapegoat. We see enough examples in the press today of stereotyping and we do not necessarily have to believe every word we read in contemporary accounts of the seaman's lot.

The *Ottawa* records tell us so much, but then fall tantalisingly silent. But in many ways the seafarer was neither hapless victim nor dangerous outsider: he was master of his own fate, whether to fall for the blandishments of the crimp or boarding house master, drink too much and get into trouble, or save his money and took a good sum home to his wife and children. Although hard and dangerous, it was clearly a way of life that many found satisfying, and which exposed the often illiterate working man to a wide range of experiences, of sights, tastes and odours, that nowadays we have to pay large sums of money to share in.

---

1   For example, 'Poor Jack. The perilous history of the merchant seaman', idem

2   'Masters Under God: Makers of Empire 1816 – 1884', Richard Woodman, The History Press 2009

3   ibid.

4   'Jack in Port' idem

5   ibid

6   'Jack in Port', Judith Fingard, University of Toronto Press 1982

7   ibid

8   ibid, also '"Those crimps of hell and goblins damned": the image and reality of Quebec's sailortown bosses' idem, and 'Working men who got wet', Proceedings of the Fourth Conference of the Atlantic Canada Shipping project, Maritime History Group Editors R Ommer and G Panting, Memorial University of Newfoundland, 1980

Chapter 10

ILLNESS, ACCIDENT AND WELLBEING ON THE *CITY OF OTTAWA*

What can the records tell us about the illnesses that mariners were subject to, and the medical care they might receive, in the second half of the 19th Century?

Of the logbooks that have survived, those of John Barrett relate to the period before the developments in medicine outlined below whereas Henry Pinhey took over in 1869 just as standards started to improve. In general the log books provide details of illness and accidents, but crew lists are less helpful as they record only if someone is left behind because of illness or death.

By the period that the *Ottawa* first went to sea, medical care for the seaman was beginning to be given serious consideration. The Seaman's Hospital Society had been founded in London in 1821, and was based at first on hospital ships but from 1870 started to transfer to land-based institution[1]. By the mid 19th Century there was a seaman's hospital in most ports. If a serious condition was identified while at sea, the sailor would be sent to hospital on reaching land where there was one, and certainly in the *Ottawa's* records we see sick mariners being sent to hospitals in Genoa and La Spezia, Italy, Moulmein, Aden, and Quebec.

When the vessel arrived in port, there could be a spate of ailments reported, sometimes because the disease might be contracted there (dysentery for instance), perhaps sometimes because the sailor had 'saved it up' as he felt it better to be treated in hospital than by the Master, or even as an opportunity to jump ship (as in the case of August José). Under a 800-year old law, when an ill or injured seaman still under articles was left behind in a hospital in a foreign port the shipowner must pay for his treatment[2]. William Wright was left behind in the hospital in Aden in May 1871, and the Master, Henry Pinhey, paid his wages, left his documents and clothes, and in addition 30 rupees for his hospital dues for one month. Local agents could provide aid, but it was mainly the responsibility of the British Consuls, who also recorded deaths at sea or serious illness, or arranged repatriation if appropriate: on 18th June 1868, passage home to his native France was arranged for Victor Duboeuf who was suffering from 'pains in his chest' by the French Consul in Aden. But sometimes people could be left behind in hospital with no money, as no wages were due to them, especially if they were considered to be undeserving because of contracting venereal disease.

At sea, however, illness and accident were within the remit of the Master, and throughout the 19th Century a series of more or less effective medical guides had been available to him. By the 1860s the medical profession was growing in confidence, and was beginning to get to grips with diagnosis and prevention of illness. The germ theory of disease, or the recognition of the importance of insects in carrying malaria and yellow fever, were still unknown, and the only really effective treatments available were mercury for syphilis (which in any case was considered too dangerous for the ship's captain to carry), and quinine for malaria. By our period cholera outbreaks were much rarer, following the observations of John Snow during the major epidemic of 1854 in Soho, who made the connection with infected water (it was previously believed that infection was through 'bad air'.) Also it was understood that malaria and yellow fever were associated with onshore swamps, and Masters were advised to anchor well away from them. Growing outcry about work and life conditions for sailors resulted in The Merchant Shipping Act of 1854 which was passed in the face of strong opposition from some ship owners who feared for their profits, and watered down its provisions as far as possible. Happily it was amended in 1867 and given more teeth.

The Ship Captain's Medical Guide

The 1867 Act stipulated that British shipowners must ensure that there was a supply of medicines, medical stores and a copy of the new Ship Captain's Medical Guide on board. This publication was found to be so useful that it has been regularly updated and is still in use today. It aimed to set out clear descriptions of symptoms and treatment for various conditions likely to be met with at sea, and put a lot of emphasis on providing a good diet, good nursing and plenty of rest. It recognised the limitations of medicine at that time, and underlined the importance of prevention, as it considered (quite realistically!) that despite the best efforts of the Master, Nature is (or was then) the best cure. Sleeping places were to be kept clean, dry and well ventilated, and forecastle, deckhouse, cabins and gallery should be thoroughly cleaned out, washed and swabbed down once a week, using carbolic acid as a disinfectant. Seamen suffering from contagious diseases should be isolated as far as possible, and sleeping areas disinfected every day. The emphasis on fresh air and cleanliness was undoubtedly beneficial in the generally crowded conditions on board

The medicine chest contained such exotically names substances as 'Opodeldoc' for rheumatism, 'Tincture of Henbane', 'Nitrate of Potash', Ipecacuanha', but the Guide recognised that it was more important to ensure good quality in a few essential and powerful drugs such as quinine and opium, as medicines at best only alleviated symptoms, and made the sailor feel that 'something was being done'. It had a somewhat nanny-like obsession with bowel movements, generally prescribing either laxatives or anti-diarrhoea medicines. Few treatments could be seen as actually dangerous or undesirable, except perhaps for urethral washouts in the treatment of gonorrhoea. The Guide definitely contributed to a reduction of infectious diseases among seamen[3].

Recognising that shipowners who feared for their profits were unlikely to fritter any of them away on seamen's health unless it was in their interests, the Guide carefully explained the financial benefits of having a healthy crew, and advised shipowners to benefit from the system of (non-compulsory) medical examinations before sailing which was set out in the Act. Nevertheless it seems many ports did not in fact appoint Medical Inspectors, and where they were in post, not many ship's captains requested them.

The Master needed a strong stomach for some of the treatments described, was expected to be able to make complicated diagnoses, to mix medicines carefully, and spend quite a lot of time making observations and carrying out treatments, if he followed all the instructions given. Nevertheless the system could be caring. People might be looked after for a considerable length of time when ill, as in the case of William Hood who hurt his neck in a fall from the topgallant forecastle. Even though it happened while the *Ottawa* was still off Liverpool, he stayed on board sick from 7th to 26th December 1870, when he was put to repairing flags as an easier task. It was only by January 4th that he returned to his duty by day, and on January 8th he returned to full duty. Despite this he sustained permanent damage, as by July he was complaining of rheumatism of the neck and was taken to the Burmese doctor.

SCURVY

It had been noticed in the 18th Century that taking citrus fruits such as lime or lemon both prevented and cured this disease, which was caused by a lack of Vitamin C in the diet, and disabled crews and could even lead to death. Consequently it had already been eliminated in the Royal Navy by 1800[4] but it proved harder to eradicate in the merchant marine, where long voyages in sailing ships with few stops in port to stock up with fresh fruit and vegetables led to many cases of crew disabled or even dying of it. The Merchant Shipping Act of 1854 required the provision of lime or lemon juice but had not resulted in much improvement, because adulterated lime juice was sometimes supplied, it could be poorly stored, and because the crew themselves could be unwilling to take it[5]. However after the amended Merchant Shipping Act of 1867, admission rates to the Dreadnought and Albert Dock Hospitals dropped rapidly[6]. An ounce was to be served out each day to every member of crew after the ship had been 10 days at sea. Crew who refused to take it were to be reported in the logbook (there were no cases of this in the *City of Ottawa* records). Moreover the quality of the lemon or limejuice was to be certified by medical officers, and mixed with 15% spirits to make it palatable, obtained from a Bonded Warehouse and accompanied by a certificate from the Inspector of the Board of Trade (sugar would also be added). Despite the stringency of these regulations cases were still reported to the Seaman's Hospital Society, but at a lesser rate. Of course other factors came into play as the century went on, in particular the prevalence of steam ships who had shorter journey times and more stops to refuel when fresh food could be taken on board. Also even good quality limejuice can deteriorate over time. Certainly in the case of the *Ottawa* the Ship's Articles from then on included the daily provision of limejuice, and there were no reported cases of the disease on board.

The *City of Ottawa* records show several main types of ailment.

Accidents

Accidents at sea were quite frequent, and were generally the result of the dangerous conditions encountered on board. In fact, it is perhaps surprising that they were not more frequent, and this is a tribute to the common sense and skills of the seamen: I myself sailed as crew on a sailing ship to get some idea of what it was like on board, and although we sailed only for a few days along the Devon coastline in good weather and with modern rigorous safety standards, even then one crew member managed to break his arm! Although the Master no doubt did his best, and the advice given by the Ship Captain's Medical Guide is sensible, accidents often resulted in long term damage.

There were two incidents of dislocated wrists: the first occurred on

November 2nd 1867, at 3.00 in the morning while at sea, when Charles Meyer (aged 22) fell against the bulwarks. The accident happened two weeks before arriving at Cardiff, so the log book does not indicate if it resulted in long term damage. A dislocated wrist also resulted when Charles Keates (31) fell from the fore rigging in 1872 in the Mediterranean and although on this occasion the Master set it, this was not very successful and Keates had to be left behind sick in La Spezia, Italy.

Bad weather was sometimes expressly the cause of the accident. On February 6th 1874, in heavy winter seas James McKae (26), who was steering, was thrown violently over the wheel and broke his right leg and kneecap. The Master put on splints and bandages immediately, but it must have been uncomfortable in the crowded and constantly moving vessel and he was taken to hospital on reaching Plymouth a fortnight later. McKae was probably lucky that the accident happened so close to port.

Unloading and loading cargo could be a dangerous occupation, as shown by the case of Antonio Jouy, aged only 17, who fell onto a raft of timber in Quebec, dislocated his kneecap and had to be left behind in the hospital, and Nicol Bain who did the same thing three years later but with less damaging results, as seven days in hospital cured him.

Sometimes the patient made a full recovery after treatment on board. While at sea on May 14th 1870, Robert Stephens (28) fell into the hold while going to get a drink of water. The precise injuries sustained aren't described but the Master 'applied medicines etc as necessary', and he returned to his duties on 11th June, a month later, quite well. He apparently had no further trouble for the rest of the voyage.

Some men only had themselves to blame: on 31st May 1868 Edward Roach (23) got into a fight onshore and 'had his lip bit' very badly but returned to work five days later. And on 30th September 1872 CV Neilsen (28) similarly returned on board from shore leave in Burma so badly hurt from fighting that he couldn't work for two days.

FEVERS, AGUES ...

Fevers, agues, dysentery, diarrhoea, bad colds arose quite frequently. The voyage of 1872/3 to Italy and Burma started badly in this respect as there was an outbreak of smallpox in London before the ship set sail: the Pall Mall Gazette[7] recorded that 'the deaths in London last week were 491 above the average, the total number being 2,121. The increase in the deaths from small-pox, which has been noticed in recent weeks, was fully maintained last week.' When the ship set out for Burma on 18th January 1872, no less than five seamen were found to be sick and were discharged at London or Plymouth before the ship reached the Atlantic: symptoms included 'bad cold and fever', and 'blindness', but three were just described as 'sick' which may have denoted smallpox: the seamen were in their twenties and early thirties. Clearly the Master, Henry Pinhey, believed that it was important to be cautious, although there were no subsequent recorded cases on board.

On the same voyage of 1872/3, by the time the vessel arrived at La Spezia in Italy in April, Richard Morrison (31) was ill with fever and ague, which recurred throughout the next six months until he was paid off in Burma, presumably because of his illness. In 1874 also John Dawson, 35, complained of fever and ague, which the Master treated with quinine. He began to be ill at sea in March, and attacks continued throughout the voyage to Doboy in the Southern United States and back. It seems likely that in both cases the seaman had contracted malaria on a previous voyage, and continued to be ill with it.

Some ports carried a particular risk of dysentery and fever. The port of Moulmein in Burma, which was situated some way from the open sea on an estuary, was particularly unhealthy in this respect, and every time the ship visited some of the crew fell sick with one or the other. The Ship Captain's Medical Guide says that dysentery 'is almost entirely confined to crews of ships trading to China and the East Indies'. It distinguishes between 9/10ths of cases which occur in port, which are easier to treat, and those which arise at sea, which are more persistent, and this is born out by the evidence from the *Ottawa*. In July 1871 at the port there was one case of dysentery, in November 1872 there was one case of fever and three of dysentery. The fever case, who was the steward, John Willcocks, 44, was sent to hospital, and had also been ill for two weeks on his previous visit there, in August 1868. The dysentery cases were treated on board and patients, aged in their 20s and 30s, recovered in a couple of days. In August 1873, there were three incidents of dysentery in Quebec, showing that this disease was not solely found in warmer seas. The men, in their twenties, were taken to hospital and one in particular took twelve days to recover.

When a case arose at sea it did indeed prove more difficult and persistent. The ship had left Moulmein in 1871 when on August 4th Edward Bellamy, 25, was laid up with dysentery, and the Master supplied him 'with the appropriate medicine and food'. He returned to work on 10th August but still had diarrhoea on 1st September, so the Master was still treating him 'according to the directions of the book'. He was getting better by 10th October and returned to work by 16th. But when the ship arrived in Plymouth at the end of December, he was discharged (before the end of the voyage) as he was still ill.

Other similar conditions included diarrhoea contracted on March 2nd 1864 in Genoa, where the seaman, aged 22, remained in hospital for a month. Ten days out of Moulmein on the same voyage of 1872/3 which seemed particularly afflicted with illness, three men fell ill with pains in the limbs and symptoms of cold, and Henry Pinhey must have been alarmed, as it was on this occasion that he recorded providing food supplements. The men, all in their twenties, recovered quickly.

More serious infectious illnesses contracted abroad that in fact resulted in death on board were 'consumption' and yellow fever.

The death attributed to consumption was that of the Bosun, William Nuttle. He had sailed on at least four voyages on the *City of Ottawa*, from 1863 – 66, and was from Plymouth. He was apparently well on the previous voyage, from which the logbook survives. But by August 8th 1866, at the age of 37, he showed the first symptoms of illness with a bowel complaint nearly two months after arriving in Bombay. If it was dysentery it was a serious attack as the doctor attended him every day but he seemed to get better by August 24th, and was well enough to sail home with the ship. Possibly this severe illness had weakened his system, as by 24th November he was sick again with cold on his chest, slowly got worse, and died on 13th January 1867 vomiting blood, the cold having turned to consumption. He was nearly back in home waters. In those days the label 'consumption' was applied to a wider and vaguer set of symptoms than the modern pulmonary tuberculosis, where the patience coughs up blood rather than vomits, with fever and breathing difficulties, so perhaps nowadays his illness would have been diagnosed differently. Nevertheless it has been estimated that up to 25% of deaths in Europe in the 19th Century were caused by TB[8]. It was not recognised that TB was caused by inhaling infected droplets, and on board ship the incidence of the disease was made worse by the living conditions of the crew, which were confined, overcrowded and damp.

Finally there were four deaths from yellow fever in 1886. The logbook for this voyage has not survived, but we can put together a lot of the details. Three men, the sailmaker, carpenter and Master, died a month after arriving in Colon, Panama, then another seaman taken on at Colon succumbed to the disease after the vessel set sail[9].

Yellow fever was endemic in South America, following its introduction from Africa – the Ship Captain's Medical Guide says that it occurs in countries where the temperature exceeds 75°F. William Lord records that when yellow fever is raging, 'you could meet someone in the morning in good health and hear they were dead by the evening.'[10] By this date, it was already recognised that early diagnosis and treatment greatly increased the chances of survival, and that for this a thermometer was essential, to detect that the patient was running a fever. However, the medical profession still felt that these instruments should not be carried by ships, because of the difficulty of interpreting them (though as Dr Carter points out, if a Captain could read a sextant he could surely read a thermometer![11]).

The vessel went through two periods of quarantine, comprising two weeks in Colon, and three weeks in New Orleans. It must have been an unpleasant and frightening experience, where the men were confined to ship and had to endure daily fumigating of both themselves and the bedding. But it was moderately effective, at least no-one else died. American quarantine rules were particularly stringent, and on October 27th 1882 the *City of Ottawa* was again held up on arriving at Pensacola in the southern USA. The Ship's Articles do not record that anyone had died, so perhaps the disease had been rife in the vessel's previous port of call, St Vincent on the Cape Verde Islands.

Various Other Problems

Sometimes it is difficult to be certain about the exact nature of the illness described, or to assess how serious it was, for instance the 'pains in the back' reported by Francis Westlake (39), the carpenter, on January 9th 1868 which kept him off work for 8 days; were these just the result of the carpenter's workload? In any case four days later he was off ill again with a swelled foot. Rheumatism was a common side effect of the seafaring life and perhaps the symptoms described were an instance of this; certainly rheumatism caused Colin McPherson (42) to be taken to hospital in Burma, for 13 days from June 21st 1871. James Summons (32) had it so badly on April 16th 1872 at La Spezia, Italy, that he was sent to hospital and was still ill when the ship sailed on 5th May, so he was left behind with his wages and clothes. At 32, he was a comparatively young man.

Other symptoms recorded include 'bad hands' which were bad enough to ensure that William Morley (34) was taken to the doctor in Pensacola in 1874: these might perhaps be grouped together with the 'boils in leg' suffered by Samuel Lacy in May 1872 which were caused, the Ship Captain's Medical Guide says, 'by the constant irritation of skin from saltwater'.

Charles Anderson (24) was taken to the doctor for his sore throat on March 25th and again on 8th April 1872 at La Spezia. By November he was laid up with pain in the limbs and the Master treated him with medicines. A more serious condition that caused the sufferer to have to leave the ship was the burst blood vessel suffered by William Wright in Aden on May 26th 1871.

Rather mysterious also is the case of death from asthma. On October 21st 1873, at the beginning of the voyage and while off the coast of Portugal, John Betty, cook, aged 50, was taken ill with this, nearly choking. He recovered enough to return to work three days later, but then on 29th died suddenly of an acute fit of it.

Asthma seems a surprising disease to die of at sea, though clearly he had a chronic condition as he carried his medication with him. One would imagine that the bracing sea air would be beneficial to the condition. No doubt the crowded sleeping conditions made it worse. This could have been a case of 'cardiac asthma', left ventrical failure rather than bronchospasm[12]. Possibly he had been invalided out of the navy, as he had just left it and returned to civilian life.

Illness as Excuse

It does seem also that illness was on occasion used as an excuse, either as a way of getting off the ship, or perhaps so the seaman could get out of work for a bit. Already mentioned is the case of Francis Osborne, 29, who requested to be allowed to go ashore to get medicines but used this as an opportunity to slip away and get drunk (the Master called his bluff and took him to a doctor, who pronounced him fit). Also that of a somewhat older rogue, August José, the 35 year old Frenchman, who having tried to jump ship but been brought back by a police launch, claimed to need a sick note for the hospital but managed to evade his captors and slipped away, never to be seen again. Also the group of five seamen, in their twenties and thirties, who had caused problems throughout the voyage of 1872/3 and who all claimed to be ill on returning to Falmouth, but on the return of the Master to the ship mysteriously got well again and proceeded on their way.

Ailments also arose as a result of mariners succumbing to some of the various temptations to bad behaviour at sea.

Drunkenness

Robert Purves, 36, joined the ship drunk on 20th September 1879, and failed to sober up over the next four days, becoming instead more sick and was left behind 'through his own default' with no wages due to him. This seems a little hard, as it sounds as though he was actually sick, or perhaps made ill by whatever he had been drinking. Moreover there was another example of a seaman apparently poisoned by alcohol, as in 1869, William Curnoe (who had been persistently drunk) was found shaking badly with the horrors and was treated with brandy.

SEXUALLY TRANSMITTED DISEASES

This is one of the most common conditions mentioned in the logbooks, which refer to them as 'the Venereal'. The Guide of 1868 takes its usual pragmatic tone, although it also says 'this disease generally appears from two days to a week after connection with a foul woman', a non-pc way of referring to the female involved, and dropped in later editions. Sailors left behind in hospital for this reason forfeited their back pay, as the Merchant Navy in general took an unsympathetic view, and it was generally considered that it was their own fault. The Ship Captain's Medical Guide advises that Shipowners and Master make use of the medical examinations of new crew provided for by the Act, and advised providing good tobacco, good beer or other liquor, and newspapers, to discourage excessive indulgence in port. The hour of shore leave should be as early as possible, and the men should go to the doctor as soon as symptoms were observed. It stated that personal cleanliness was one of the best means of prevention. It was only in the 1940s that it was recognised that venereal disease was always going to be a hazard for sailors, and they received advice on prevention, and the use of condoms, rather than blame.

Ten cases specifically identified as venereal disease are noted in the logbooks, which do not really distinguish in general between syphilis, which was difficult to control, gonorrhoea, which could be resolved, and other genital infections. Perhaps most interesting is the case of Henry Tiltman, apprentice, aged 17, who, on March 2nd 1864, was sent to hospital in Genoa with the disease. When the ship was ready to put to sea on 11th April, the doctor said he was not yet fit and would not be for a fortnight or three weeks, so by the advice of the consul he was left behind in hospital. It seems he went on to make a full recovery, married, transferred to the Royal Navy then retired to his native village, and went on to have 2 sons and enjoy a long married life, dying at 73 of cerebral thrombosis and cancer of the tongue. Possibly his illness resolved itself, either because of and in spite of the treatment he received, as he would not have been accepted in the Navy if he had any overt signs of venereal disease. Otherwise he may have simply transmitted it to his wife and children, which according to Dr Carter 'was not an uncommon situation in 19th Century Britain'.[13]

All other seafarers who were identified with venereal disease were in their twenties or early thirties. They generally went to hospital or were treated on board for symptoms, which were suppressed but then often recurred. Perhaps inevitably most of the sufferers were also the crewmembers who were most in trouble for leaving the ship without leave or coming back drunk.

CAUSES OF DEATH AMONG THE CREW

As well as those who died while sailing on the *Ottawa*, it has been possible within the remit of this research to find out the causes of death of some of the crewmembers, mainly Masters, who died after leaving the vessel.

Deaths at Sea

As mentioned above, the causes of deaths recorded on board the *City of Ottawa* comprise infectious disease – 'consumption' and yellow fever: chronic disease – asthma: and accident. There was also the death of Frederick Withycombe, one of the first Masters of the vessel who died on the passage back from Calcutta, India in 1861 at the age of 54, cause unknown, but conceivably of disease contracted overseas.

It has been possible to trace a further five deaths at sea subsequent to leaving the vessel. There is one case of shipwreck, that of William Bunker, long time Mate on the *Ottawa*, who was drowned when the *Wyre* was run down in the English Channel at the age of 49 in 1884. William Dunn died of apoplexy at the age of 38 while Master of the *James Duncan* in 1882 at Santos, Brazil. He was young to suffer a heart attack or stroke, but it might have been linked to stress arising from the pressures of his job, from overindulgence in food or wine, or just to cardiac weakness. Thomas Restarick, former owner of the *Ottawa*, died of dropsy sailing as an ordinary seaman on board the *Jessie Readman* at the age of 43 in 1878. 'Dropsy' is one of the vaguer Victorian diagnoses but was probably the result of kidney failure, rather than any particular lifestyle factors, though perhaps disappointment played a part, as the experience of running the *Ottawa* and other sailing ships seems to have ruined him financially. John Barrett died at Queenstown, Ireland, in 1877 on board the *Ribble* at the age of 46, cause of death not recorded. Another Master James Melrose drowned at sea somewhere off Newcastle Upon Tyne while Mate of the *John O'Scott* in 1894, age 56.

Deaths on Land

Those who subsequently died on land did not necessarily die peaceful deaths.

As we have seen, Henry Pinhey, in debt and alcoholic, committed suicide by throwing himself into the harbour in Quebec at the age of 67 in 1901. Evidently, like most sailors, he could not swim. Frederick Lyle, who was going to sail as Master of the *Ottawa* in March 1879, but had to leave after one day because of sickness, suffered a somewhat similar fate. He never it seems recovered his health and was found drowned in the River Avon at Bristol nearly two years later at the age of 52 in mysterious circumstances. He also had an alcohol problem. Probably also related to lifestyle choices was the death of Frederick Pinhey, brother of Henry, who sailed as Boson and Second Mate on the *Ottawa*. He died suddenly in 1883 at the age of 37 of 'rupture of blood vessel of the lungs' which could well have been linked to heavy smoking or the more common chewing tobacco, or of course the general dampness of the seafaring life. Similarly Master Thomas Hellyer Bootyman lived to the grand age of 79 and died at home with his family around him, but it was of acute bronchitis, surely the result of his long life at sea.

Finally some died at home in old age of conditions apparently unrelated to their seagoing years: Thomas Armitage Jackson succumbed to cystitis at the age of 72, Henry Tiltman was 73 when he died of cerebral thrombosis and cancer of the tongue, and Joseph George Jury lived to the age of 82 when he succumbed to a cerebral haemorrhage.

Time of Death Unknown

Although it hasn't always been possible to trace when seafarers died, it is easier to find out when they last went to sea. As far as can be traced, this is a list of the remaining Masters, plus one other officer:

Robert Martin sailed to the age of 66. Samuel Lewis disappears from history at 39, when he either died or, leaving his old family behind, created a new life for himself in America, which was not an unusual proceeding at the time. James Robertson sailed to 54, James Hatfield to 48, and the steward, John Willcocks, continued to at least 62.

CONCLUSIONS

It has been estimated that in the mid-19th Century most crews of foreign going ships were in poor health by the time they reached 35/40, with an average life expectancy of 45 years[14]. This is hard to test from the *Ottawa*'s records, as the majority of the crew were always in their 20s and 30s. Although many did continue longer, many others seem to have given up the nautical life when they had satisfied a need for adventure and wanted to settle down. And many just disappear from the historical records.

Furthermore there are so many imponderables: what exactly is meant, in modern terms, by some of the vague descriptions of ailments? When men were left behind seriously ill in hospital, did they go on to make a full recovery, as Henry Tiltman apparently did, or did they die, or spend the rest of their life with a disability? Any conclusions offered have to be tentative.

However with the above reservations we can conclude that over a ten year period seven men, probably eight, suffered accidents while sailing on the *Ottawa* which caused death or definitely or probably affected their quality of life, five of them while aged 31 or less. Five had accidents from which they recovered. Possibly twelve men under 40 caught infectious diseases from which they either died or suffered from debilitating or chronic symptoms which were likely to affect their quality of life (this includes the four cases of yellow fever which occurred outside the period covered by the logbooks) while 12 more cases were successfully treated either in hospital or on board. Seven of the eight recorded cases of Sexually Transmitted Diseases were similarly likely to have long-term detrimental effects on the seamen's health. Thirteen men were reported with various other debilitating or fatal illnesses, and there were perhaps a further ten cases of conditions successfully treated. So over the ten years of the log books, we might estimate that there were 35 serious or terminal cases, out of the perhaps 300 men who served as crew in that time, most affecting men in their twenties or thirties, who in any case made up the majority of the crew. Twenty-six cases were treated successfully. A recent report[15] found that among Danish fishermen in the 1990s there were 20.4 work related injuries per 100 men at sea, which interestingly is not a dissimilar figure.

Many of the ailments reported were directly connected to the seafaring lifestyle, including infectious diseases contracted overseas (malaria, yellow fever), accidents resulting from the dangerous operations of climbing the rigging, loading or unloading the cargo, or stormy weather, also rheumatism, bronchitis and chronic chest infections and painful skin conditions. Less directly linked but still a hazard of the job were venereal disease and alcoholism, which we know afflicted at least some of the retired sea captains.

Based on the information we have on officers, we see that many of their deaths were likewise directly or indirectly a legacy of their seafaring life (Dunn, Frederick Pinhey, Henry Pinhey, perhaps Thomas Restarick, Frederick

Lyle, Thomas Bootyman) or shipwreck or accident at sea (Bunker, Melrose), and we see some early deaths under 50 (Barrett, Bunker, Frederick Pinhey). Nevertheless many continued to pursue their career into their 50s or even 60s, and some lived to their seventies, which was a very good age at the time. It is probable that officers had a better lifestyle, less dangerous work and better nutrition than the ordinary seaman, so we might perhaps expect them to live longer, although on the other hand every Master who served on the *Ottawa* had started as 'boy' or apprentice and worked his way up, and was as much at risk of infectious disease and shipwreck as the ordinary seamen.

Although the records relating to the *City of Ottawa* do not provide a big enough sample to generalise from, they give an interesting snapshot of life at sea, and it is possible to come to some tentative conclusions. In many ways despite the particular hazards, seafarers did not have it so bad. Merchant seamen had access to sensible if basic health care at all times, and to hospital care when in port, and probably stood a better chance of recovering from illness or accident than the land-based working man who did not have such access. At the start of the our period, in 1860, large towns were very unhealthy with frequent epidemics of cholera, typhoid and typhus, and it was only after this date that conditions slowly improved due to the installation of sewerage systems, better and less overcrowded housing and cleaner water. In 1851 a boy born in inner Liverpool had a life expectancy of only 26 years[16]. Nor could city dwellers expect to have such ready access to hospital care. Through much of our period, life on board ship was probably rather healthier than life in a Victorian city, with the added bonuses of an exciting life and foreign travel!

1. 'Disease in the Merchant Navy. A history of the Seamen's Hospital Society', Gordon C Cook, Radcliffe Publishing, 2007
2. "'The Ship Captain's Medical Guide' and the management of infectious disease at sea 1867 – 1967", unpublished MA Thesis, Dr John Timothy Carter, Greenwich Maritime Institute. I am very grateful to Dr Carter for comments and advice on the more technical aspects of medicine
3. ibid
4. ibid
5. 'Scurvy in the British Mercantile Marine in the 19th century, and the contribution of the Seamen's Hospital Society', G C Cook, Postgraduate Medical Journal, Vol 80 2004
6. ibid
7. Pall Mall Gazette, December 20th 1871, The British Newspaper Archive (www.britishnewspaperarchive.co.uk)
8. Article in 'The Times' January 21st 2012
9. The Northern Echo, April 28th 1887, The British Newspaper Archive (www.britishnewspaperarchive.co.uk)
10. 'Reminiscences of a sailor', William R Lord, Historical Collection of the British Library, 1894
11. Personal communication from Dr Carter
12. ibid
13. ibid
14. A G Course, 'The Merchant Navy, a Social History', A G Course, Frederick Muller Ltd, London, 1963, quoted in G C Cook, idem
15. 'Work related injuries in Danish fishermen', O L Jensen, in The Journal of Occupational Medicine, Vol 46, No 6, pp 414-420, 1996
16. Victorian Britain, bbc.co.uk/history

Chapter 11

CONCLUSIONS

Writing this book has been a long and fascinating journey, and the evidence points to some interesting and in some cases quite surprising conclusions. The first thing which may be said is what a small world it actually was, with the same names so often cropping up at different places and in different connections.

ORDINARY SEAMEN

As we have seen, most men who went to sea were young men, who spent a year or a few years getting their lust for adventure out of their veins before settling down (as in the case of Wilcocks' son Samuel). Some unfortunately had a less happy experience by suffering an accident or illness, but their chances of recovering were good, compared to that of working class landsmen. Perhaps a tenth of merchant seamen might die or have their lifestyle seriously impaired in their twenties or thirties, a proportion which is very close to work-related injuries for Danish fishermen in the 1990s. But many lived to a good age. Far from being rootless vagrants, most career seamen had a wife and family, as was the case of Nuttle, Willcocks, Betty and others whom it has been possible to trace. On the other hand, those determined to misbehave were also the ones most likely to desert and although we can certainly detect the signs of crimps at work, seamen were free to make their own decisions as to whether to desert or not and most did not.

What is particularly surprising is how fluid society was, and how it was quite possible to progress in a nautical career. Even ordinary seamen could have a good education – we remember John Betty the cook's books – although many did not. It was perfectly possible for a boy from a poor non-nautical background with brains and application to progress up the career ladder to Bosun and even to Master – as did William Dunn and George Griffin.

Masters

So going to sea was a good career for working class or lower middle class boys, although it seems that it was usually the elder son who was most successful. While some progressed on merit, it is certain that some were helped by family or local connections. Most had a strong sense of family – Pinhey, Barrett, Willcocks, Martin, all had family members who sailed with them or visited them. Lyle, Bootyman, Jackson, Pinhey all retired to live with their families. It was quite a frequent pattern for seafarers to marry and have children later in life, for instance William Barrett, Samuel James Hatfield, Frederick William Withycombe. At the beginning of the period, the seafaring career was passed down from father to son – Bootyman, Barrett, Hatfield, Tiltman, Withycombe all had relatives who went to sea or had shore-based maritime jobs, or had children who followed them to sea. However by the end of the century the children of the largest proportion of mariners went into a totally different career: William Barrett, Bootyman, Samuel Lewis, Henry Tiltman, Frederick Lyle all had children who preferred to stay on dry land.

The job was not without its reverses – nearly every Master experienced at least one shipwreck. Some apparently found this traumatic, as was the case with Robertson. In later life some Masters either preferred to work as Mates or were unable to get a position as Master. And a high proportion of them died in a way either directly or indirectly linked to their lifestyle.

Financial Success

It was clearly possible for a Master to make a satisfactory profit from his work as we see from the not inconsiderable personal fortunes that some of them left in their wills, which gave them quite a respectable position in society. The ordinary seaman could also bring home a reasonable living if he was careful, and amass a quantity of treasured possessions as in the case of Bunker, though the families of some were living in very poor surroundings.

By and large shipowners did not appear to do well out of their investment. Although the first Thomas Restarick apparently prospered, his son did not and JP Rogers seems to have been in desperate financial straits by the end. By the end of the century an elderly sailing ship could not really pay its way, but part of the reason why the *Ottawa* was so unprofitable for her owners can be detected in the patterns of her journeys. The lack of a centralised system of distribution or good communications meant that she often sailed in one direction in ballast, halving profits. Because after her first few years she specialised in heavy goods, timber, coal and pig iron, she found it hard to get a cargo in many British ports, but it was also a weakness of some British trading ports that they tended to specialise in certain limited areas: as was the case of Cardiff, for instance.

AND FINALLY ...

A final thought is that women have not really cropped up much in this narration, but we do get a glimpse of the lives of sailor's wives, sometimes going to sea with her husband, but often bringing up a young family virtually alone, waiting for the next injection of money when (if) their husbands come ashore again with no way of communicating major events to him, and very little chance to get news of his progress. They often lived with relatives, or in crowded tenements with a whole community of other sailor's wives. On the other hand, we see that a loving father like Henry Pinhey usually contrived to get home to his daughter around Christmas time. With which thought, worthy of a book by Jane Austen, we leave the *City of Ottawa*, hoping that her venerable timbers will one day be treated with the respect they deserve and not left to slowly rot away where they lie.

BIBLIOGRAPHY

ARTICLES

Arminas D, 'The sailing ship – *City of Ottawa*', Argonautica, the newsletter of the Canadian Nautical Research Society, Vol XXVI, No 1 Jan 2009

Benoît J, 'Grandeur et déclin de la construction navale à Québec', Cap-aux-Diamants: la revue d'histoire du Québec, no 22, 1990, pp 47-50

Blocksidge BW, 'Hints on the Register Tonnage of Merchant Ships', The Journal of Commerce, Charles Birchall and Sons 1933

Brayshay M, 'Plymouth's past: so worthy and peerless a western port' in 'Plymouth. Maritime City in Transition', ed B Chalkley, D Dunkerley, P Gripaios, Polytechnic South West 1991

Brown I and Gale F, 'The *City of Ottawa* - the remains of a Nineteenth Century Full Rigged Ship lying in the Foryd Harbour, Rhyl, North Wales', Flintshire Historic Society Journal, 2007, pp 87 – 105

Carter JT, "The Ship's Captain's Medical Guide" and the management of infectious disease at sea 1867 – 1967', unpublished MA Thesis, Greenwich Maritime Institute

Carter JT, 'Infections at sea past and present', editorial to the published papers for the International Maritime Health Association workshop, 'Infectious diseases in the twenty-first century', held at Singapore in November/December 2009

Fingard J, "Those crimps of hell and goblins damned": the image and reality of Quebec's sailortown bosses' in 'Working men who got wet', The Maritime History Group ed R Ommer and G Panting. The Proceedings of the 4th Conference of the Atlantic Canada Shipping Project, Memorial University of Newfoundland 1980

Gifford, 'Rhyl Foryd Harbour. An assessment of the wreck – *City of Ottawa*', Report No. 14533 RO1a, December 2007

Gifford, 'Rhyl Foryd Harbour. A survey of the wreck – *City of Ottawa*', Report No. 14533 RO3, July 2008

Jensen OL, 'Work related injuries in Danish fishermen', Journal of Occupational Medicine, Vol 46, No 6, 1996 pp 414 - 420

Patterson G, 'The Shipping Industry: life and death at sea', in 'The Great Age of Industry in the North East' ed RW Sturgess, Durham County Local History Society 1981

Samuel J, 'Shipshape in French', The Linguist, Vol 53, No 4 2014 p24

Samuel J, 'Ancient Mariners', Mensa Magazine, August 2014

Samuel J, 'Illness, Accident and Wellbeing on the *City of Ottawa* ', Flintshire Historic Society Journal, 2007, *upcoming*

Stammers M, 'Iron knees in wooden vessels – an attempt at a typology', International Journal of Nautical Archaeology, Vol 30 (1), 2001, pp 115 - 121

Van Driel A, 'Tonnage Measurement, a historic and critical essay', The Hague Government Printing Office 1925

Wessex Archaeology, '*City of Ottawa*, Foryd Harbour, Rhyl, Denbighshire, North Wales. Undesignated Site Assessment. Unpublished Report. 53111.02-7, 2011, pps i-ii

BOOKS

Burns JM, 'The life and times of a merchant sailor. The archaeology and history of the merchant ship *Catharine*', Kluwer Academic/Plenum Publishers 2003

Conway-Jones H, 'The Gloucester and Sharpness Canal. An illustrated history', Amberley Publishing plc 2009

Cook GC, 'Scurvy in the British Mercantile Marine in the 19th century, and the contribution of the Seamen's Hospital Society', Postgraduate Medical Journal, Vol 80 2004

Cook GC, 'Disease in the Merchant Navy. A history of the Seamen's Hospital Society', Radcliffe Publishing 2007

A G Course, 'The Merchant Navy, a Social History', Frederick Muller Ltd, London, 1963, quoted in G C Cook, 'Scurvy in the British Mercantile Marine' idem

Fingard J, 'Jack in Port', University of Toronto Press 1982

Forwood WB, 'Reminiscences of a Liverpool Shipowner 1850 – 1920', General Books, originally published 1920

Greenhill B, 'The ship. The life and death of the merchant sailing ship', Her Majesty's Stationary Office, 1980

Greenhill B, 'The Evolution of the Wooden Ship', The Blackburn Press 1988

Greenhill B and Giffard A, 'The Merchant Sailing Ship: A Photographic History', David and Charles, Newton Abbot 1970

Harris DW, 'Maritime History of Rhyl and Rhuddlan', Prints and Pictures 1991

Hedges AAC, 'East Coast Shipping', Shire Publications Lts 1974

Hicks GE, 'Plymouth's other fleet – the Merchant Shipping Registers of the Port of Plymouth', unpublished CD

Hope R, 'Poor Jack. The perilous history of the merchant seaman', Chatham Publishing London 2001

Hydrographic Department of the Admiralty, 'Ocean Passages of the World' 1895

Lord WR, 'Reminiscences of a sailor', Historical Collection of the British Library 1894

Lubbock B, 'The Log of the Cutty Sark', Brown, Son at Ferguson Ltd 1994

Marcil ER, 'On chantait "Charley-Man". La construction de grands voiliers à Québec de 1763 à 1893', Les Éditions GID, 2000

National Geospatial Intelligence Agency, Bethesda, Maryland, 'Sailing Directions (enroute): East Coast of Australia and New Zealand', Publication 127, US Government 2010

Plimsoll S, 'Our Seamen. An Appeal', Virtue and Co, London 1873, reprinted by Kenneth Mason, Havant, Hampshire

Richie-Noakes N, 'Liverpool's Historic Waterfront. The world's first mercantile dock system', HMSO 1984

Samuel J, 'Le *City of Ottawa*: l'histoire d'un grand voilier en bois', Éditions GID, *upcoming*

Vallières M, 'Québec: les regions de Québec, histoire en bref', Les Presses de l'Université Laval 2010

Villiers A, 'Square-rigged ships: an introduction', National Maritime Museum, Greenwich London 2009

Villiers P, 'Joseph Conrad, Master Mariner', Seafarer Books 2006

Woodman R, 'Masters under God. Makers of Empire 1816 – 1884' in A History of the British Merchant Navy Vol 3', The History Press 2009

Index

Aden, 11, 36, 37, 46, 50, 51, 141, 141, 142, 149

Apprentice, 14, 16, 34, 35, 58, 66, 67, 83, 87, 91, 104-7, 114, 120, 121, 150, 154

Australia, 14, 22, 36, 60, 67, 77, 78, 79, 92

Barrett, Charles, 27, 33, 49, 103, 104, 106

Barrett, George, 33, 44, 47, 74, 114, 115

Barrett, John, 27, 28, 31-3, 35-44, 54, 57, 61, 63, 67, 77, 103-7, 109, 114-6, 120, 122, 124, 132, 136, 151, 154, 158

Barrett, William, 40, 41, 44, 47-9, 114, 115, 132, 158

Barrow, 66-68, 71, 74, 89, 91, 92

Betty, John, 39, 58, 59, 119, 124, 125, 134, 149, 157

Bombay (Mumbai), 33, 34, 46, 72, 105, 119, 147

Bootyman, Thomas Hellyer, 89, 90, 152, 154, 158

Bunker, William, 27, 33, 41-3, 57, 60, 72, 78, 83, 115, 117, 118, 124, 126, 151, 154, 158

C and J Sharples and Co, 11, 12

Calcutta, 13-17, 21, 22, 29, 151

Cape Verde and St Vincent, 16, 35, 46-8, 73, 75, 105, 122, 126, 130, 137, 148

Cardiff, 31, 35-7, 46, 47, 61, 65, 68, 71, 74, 75, 81, 84, 92, 108, 111, 123, 132, 136, 137, 145, 159

Carrier Dove, 17, 19-21, 23, 25, 27, 65, 92

Coal, 3, 11, 22, 31, 33, 35, 37, 46, 47, 50, 51, 56, 57, 60, 61, 64, 66, 67, 68, 71, 74, 75, 77, 78, 81, 89, 90-2, 108, 112, 126, 135, 159

Conrad, Joseph, 79, 105

Crimps, 2, 43, 48, 67, 70, 74, 75, 132, 133, 135, 136, 137, 157

Cutty Sark, 1, 53, 78, 90, 127

Desertion, 58, 73, 108, 130, 134, 135, 137

Dowie, Kenneth McKenzie, 12-15, 21, 23, 25

Drunk, Drunkenness, 2, 42, 44, 51, 53-5, 57, 61, 67, 70, 91, 126, 127, 128, 131, 132, 136-8, 149, 150, 151

Dunn, William, 31-3, 39, 54, 63, 64, 67-70, 73, 75, 77, 89, 104, 105, 110, 121, 136, 151, 153, 158

Dysentery, 51, 56, 57, 121, 141, 145-7

Eliza, 21, 27, 28, 30, 31, 54, 105, 115

Eliza Bencke, 15, 21, 42

Falmouth, 43, 44, 48, 53, 56, 122, 149

Forbes, William, 12

Gingras, Jean-Elie, 5-7, 9, 88

Gloucester, 47, 64, 84, 161

Greenock, 28, 60, 66, 77, 83, 129

Griffin, George, 39, 43, 54, 64, 67, 70, 78, 79, 81, 84, 85, 90, 122, 158

Hatfield, Samuel James, 11, 50, 152, 158

HMS *Fearless*, 97, 98, 100

Hodge, William Chapell, 51

Hospital, 5, 6, 31, 37, 42, 48, 49, 54, 56-8, 121, 126, 135, 141, 142, 144, 145-51, 153, 154

Jackson, Thomas Armitage, 15, 17, 21-3, 29, 38, 42, 152, 158

Jury, Joseph George, 66, 67, 120, 152

La Spezia, Italy, 53-6, 126, 137, 141, 145, 146, 148

Lewis, Samuel, 81-3, 104, 152, 158

Liverpool, 11-15, 17, 19-23, 27, 28, 34, 34, 46, 47, 49, 50, 54, 64-6, 68, 71, 87, 89, 90, 92, 116, 129, 131, 132, 135, 143, 154

London, 14, 22, 25, 29, 33, 40, 47, 52, 53, 55, 57, 58, 60, 65, 66, 73, 74, 77, 90, 122, 132, 141, 145, 146

Lyle, Frederick, 69, 70, 113, 152, 154, 158

Martin, Robert, 92, 93, 152, 158

Melrose, James, 87, 89, 91, 113, 151, 154

Moulmein, Burma, 37, 51, 53, 54, 56, 73, 74, 134, 136-8, 141, 146, 147

Newcastle, New South Wales, 77, 78

Newcastle-upon-Tyne, 47, 53, 56, 57, 83, 87, 87, 89, 151

Newport, 28, 31-3, 65, 72, 77, 80, 130

Nimrod, 57, 69, 84

Nuttle, William, 34, 38, 121, 124, 125, 134, 147, 157

Panama – Colon and Aspinwall, 46, 81, 84, 147, 148

Pensacola, USA, 39, 58, 59, 64, 68, 68, 70, 71, 73, 75, 77, 108, 111, 125, 131, 134, 148

Pinhey, Alice, 108, 109, 111, 114

Pinhey, Frank, 41, 44, 47, 48, 50, 60, 64, 107, 114, 126

Pinhey, Frederick, 41, 50, 53, 56, 57, 58, 60, 69, 107, 114, 115, 152, 153, 154

Pinhey, Henry, 32, 33, 38, 41-5, 47, 48, 50, 51, 54-9, 61-3, 89, 103, 104-6, 109-12, 114-6, 120-4, 130, 132, 132, 135, 137, 138, 141, 146, 147, 152-4, 158, 159

Pinhey, Louisa, 57, 58, 108, 108, 109, 111, 114

Plymouth, 27-35, 39, 41, 43, 44, 46, 48, 49, 51, 53, 54, 57, 58, 59, 60, 63, 67, 69-71, 72, 74, 74, 75, 80, 84, 89, 89, 104-8, 112, 114-6, 118, 120, 122, 132, 145-7

Portland, 30, 93, 94, 96

Quarantine, 71, 81, 82, 135, 136, 148

Quebec, 3, 5-9, 11-13, 22, 27, 28, 30-2, 35, 42-6, 48, 49, 57, 58, 60, 61, 63, 64, 66, 67, 73, 74, 87-92, 105, 108-12, 114, 116, 121-3, 129-31, 133-8, 141, 145, 146, 152

Restarick, Thomas and Thomas Brown, 7, 27-33, 35, 43, 50, 51, 54, 105-7, 115, 120, 130, 151, 153, 158

Rheumatism, 51, 143, 148, 153

Rhyl, 1, 3, 4, 8, 96-100

Rhyl Journal, 99

Rio di Janeiro, 16, 22, 46, 64, 68, 71, 73, 74, 77, 123, 129, 134

Robert Jones and Co, 96, 97

Robertson, James, 87, 116, 152, 158

Rogers, John Portas, 30, 52, 57, 69, 78, 81, 83, 84, 87, 90, 92, 120, 122, 158

Rooparell, 21, 22

Ross, James Gibb, 6, 7, 12, 13, 88

Ross, John, 58

Royal Navy, The, 1, 15, 29, 31, 49, 58, 90, 144, 150

Scurvy, 38, 105, 143

Sharpness, 64, 65

Ship Captain's Medical Guide, 142, 144, 146-8, 150, 155, 160

Shipbuilding, 3, 5, 6, 8, 9, 33, 88, 97

St Lawrence River, 5, 22, 28, 30, 32, 42, 44, 45, 88, 110

Steven, William, 90, 91

Suez Canal, 11, 51, 55

Tattoos, 12, 15, 104, 119

Theft, 49, 53, 54, 137

Tiltman, Henry, 31, 104, 121, 150, 152, 153, 158

Timber, 3, 5, 10-12, 28, 32, 44, 46-9, 56, 60, 64-8, 71, 75, 80, 83, 87, 88, 90, 91, 96, 100, 104, 108, 135, 145, 159

Tucker, HA or TA, 15

Willcocks, John, 38, 43, 54-6, 72, 74, 75, 115, 119, 122, 124, 146, 152, 157, 158

Willcocks, Samuel, 71

Withycombe, Frederick William, 14, 15, 24, 50, 104, 151, 158, 165

Withycombe, William Frederick, 14

Wyre, 78, 83, 116-8, 151

Yellow fever, 75, 81, 83, 136, 142, 147, 151, 153

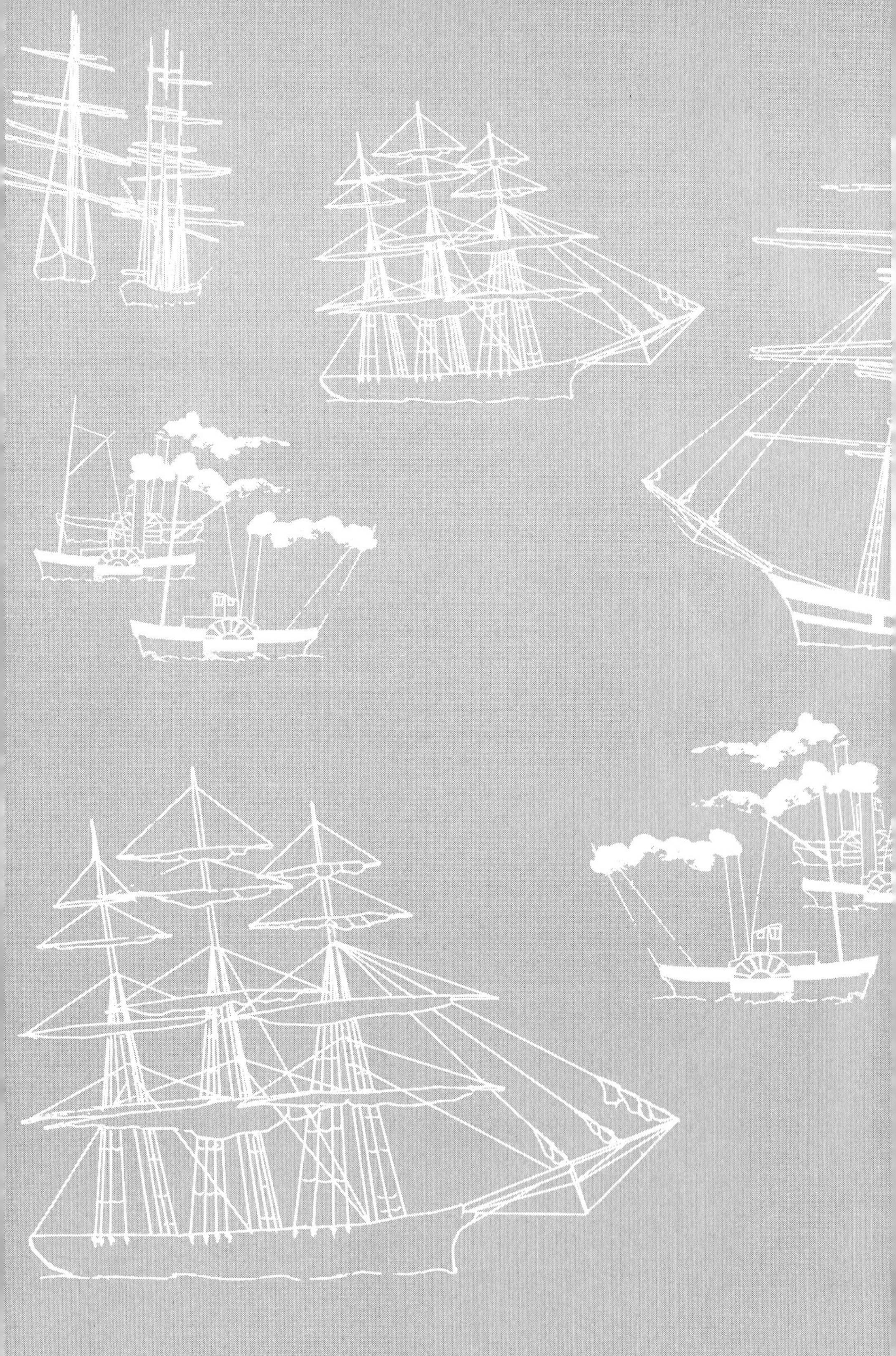